PRAYING GOD'S WILL

for
My Daughter

LEE ROBERTS

OLIVER
NELSON

THOMAS NELSON PUBLISHERS
Nashville

This book is dedicated to my daughters, Rhonda and Faith.

Other books by Lee Roberts

Praying God's Will for My Husband
Praying God's Will for My Son

Copyright © 1993 by Lee Roberts

Published in Nashville, Tennessee, by Thomas Nelson, Inc.

The Bible version used in this publication is THE NEW KING JAMES VERSION. Copyright © 1979, 1980, 1982, Thomas Nelson, Inc., Publishers. Verses have been modified to fit the prayer format.

Printed in the United States of America.

Library of Congress Cataloging-in-Publication Data

Roberts, Lee, 1941–
    Praying God's will for my daughter / Lee Roberts.
      p.   cm.
    ISBN 0-7852-7543-6 (hc)
    ISBN 0-8407-9174-7 (pbk.)
    1. Parents—Prayer-books and devotions—English. 2. Daughters—
Religious life. 3. Prayer—Christianity. I. Title.
BV283.C5R63   1993
242'.845—dc20
                                     93-9639
                                     CIP

12 13 14 15 16 17 18 — 01 00 99 98

Contents

For Parents Only   v

ANGER   1

ATTITUDE   7

CONDEMNED   12

CONFIDENCE   20

CONFUSED   25

COURAGE   32

DELIVERANCE   39

DEPRESSED   44

DESERTED BY LOVED ONES   51

DISCOURAGED   57

DISSATISFIED   63

DISTRESS / SADNESS   68

DON'T UNDERSTAND GOD   75

DOUBTING GOD   82

EMOTIONALLY UPSET   88

FAITH   96

FEAR   109

FINANCIAL PROBLEMS   116

FORGIVENESS   124

GODLY LIFE   130

GOD'S LOVE   149

GOD'S WORD   154

GRIEF / HURTING   162

INHERITANCE   170

LONELY   176

LOVE   182

LOVE FOR MY DAUGHTER   190

NEEDS   195

OBEDIENCE   201

PATIENCE   207

PEACE   214

POWER   219

PRAISE   224

PROTECTION   232

REBELLIOUS   235

SALVATION   241

SATAN DEFEATED   247

SECURITY   260

SERVING GOD   265

SICKNESS   272

SPIRITUAL GROWTH   278

STRENGTH   283

TEMPTED   289

TROUBLES   297

WAITING ON GOD   304

WORRIED   309

For Parents Only

As Christian parents, we have a solemn obligation to constantly, and on a day-by-day basis, lift up our daughter in prayer. We have a tremendous responsibility before God on her behalf. We are responsible before God for her spiritual, emotional, and physical well-being for as long as she is under our control. We are also responsible before God to give her our loving and prayerful support in order to nurture her on her journey to adulthood.

The question now becomes, "What do I pray?" As Christians, our role model for prayer must be Jesus. Jesus said, our daughter "shall not live by bread alone, but by every word that proceeds from the mouth of God" (Matthew 4:4). And the "sword of the Spirit ... is the word of God" (Ephesians 6:17).

What should you pray for your daughter? Scripture is clear that you should pray God's word for her. At the same time, you must never forget that God is sovereign and that He is not obligated to a name-it-and-claim-it theology. God will always do what is best for your daughter. But at the same time you will do well to understand that when you pray God's word for your daughter, you are actually praying both the mind and the perfect will of God for her.

If you follow a systematic plan of praying God's will for your daughter, you will see dynamic growth take place in her life, and she will become the daughter God intended her to be.

1

ANGER

12·30·15 for Catie I love you so much!

Heavenly Father, I thank You for all that You do for my daughter and me. During this time of being alone with You I ask You, in Jesus' name, to hear Your word as my prayers concerning any anger that may abide in my daughter. Your word is clear that anger does not produce the righteousness that You want in each of us. I petition You now, with Your very words, to remove any anger from my daughter that may be a stumbling block in her walk with You. Thank You, God, for answering this prayer for my daughter.

God, in accordance with Your Word...

I pray that my daughter will be swift to hear, slow to speak, slow to wrath; for her wrath does not produce the righteousness of God.

JAMES 1:19–20

I pray that the discretion of my daughter makes her slow to anger, and it is to her glory to overlook a transgression.

PROVERBS 19:11

———— ● ————

I pray that my daughter will commit her way to You, LORD, and trust also in You, and You shall bring it to pass. You shall bring forth her righteousness as the light, and her justice as the noonday. I pray that she will rest in You, LORD, and wait patiently for You. I pray that she does not fret because of someone who prospers or because of someone who brings wicked schemes to pass. I pray that she will cease from anger, and forsake wrath; that she does not fret—it only causes harm.

PSALM 37:5–8

———— ● ————

I pray that my daughter will not hasten in her spirit to be angry, for anger rests in the bosom of fools.

ECCLESIASTES 7:9

I pray that my daughter will let all bitterness, wrath, anger, clamor, and evil speaking be put away from her, with all malice. I pray also that she will be kind to others, tenderhearted, forgiving others, just as God in Christ also forgave her.

EPHESIANS 4:31–32

———— ● ————

I pray that my daughter understands that a fool vents all his feelings, but a wise person holds hers back.

PROVERBS 29:11

———— ● ————

I pray that my daughter knows that being slow to anger is better than the mighty and ruling her spirit is better than one who takes a city.

PROVERBS 16:32

———— ● ————

I pray that my daughter realizes that a person who is quick-tempered acts foolishly.

PROVERBS 14:17

Praying God's Will for My Daughter

I pray that if my daughter is angry, she will not sin. That she does not let the sun go down on her wrath.

EPHESIANS 4:26

———— ● ————

I pray that my daughter will make no friendship with an angry person and with a furious person she does not go, lest she learn their ways and set a snare for her soul.

PROVERBS 22:24–25

———— ● ————

I pray that my daughter always remembers that a soft answer turns away wrath, but a harsh word stirs up anger.

PROVERBS 15:1

4

Kitty what an amazing privilege to pray God's word over you. Praying His word in and over and thru your life. He loves us so much — He gave His only son, Christ Jesus!

You are going thru a great trial — Your heart is torn — You love 2 boys. God who created you knows you so well baby. Please trust Him, open your heart to Him and let Him in.

All of these verses I prayed tonight for you are about Anger. Let go of it! That anger its holding you back... release it, it's done way to much damage. You are so loved and treasured and cherished. I prayed these specific verses and stand in awe of our great & mighty God who is faithful. He will complete the work He began in you.

Philippians 1:6

2

ATTITUDE 1·1·2016

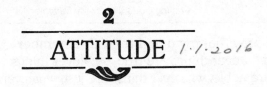

Lord Jesus, I ask You now, using the very words that have been given to me in the Holy Scriptures, to make certain that my daughter always has an attitude of joy in You and an attitude and an expectancy that she can do all things through You who gives her Your strength to face the issues and problems of life. Thank You, Lord, for her happiness and her joy. In Your name I pray. Amen.

God, in accordance with Your Word . . .

I pray that my daughter knows that she can do all things through Christ who strengthens her.

PHILIPPIANS 4:13

———— ● ————

I pray that my daughter will not sorrow, for the joy of the LORD is her strength.

NEHEMIAH 8:10

I pray that my daughter will remember
whatever things are true, whatever things
are noble, whatever things are just, whatever
things are pure, whatever things are lovely,
whatever things are of good report, if there
is any virtue and if there is anything praiseworthy—that she will meditate on these
things.

PHILIPPIANS 4:8

●

I pray that my daughter will always love You,
the Lord her God, with all her heart, with
all her soul, with all her mind, and with all
her strength and that she will love her
neighbor as herself.

MARK 12:30–31

●

I pray that my daughter will remember that
this is the day the LORD has made and that
she will rejoice and be glad in it.

PSALM 118:24

I pray that my daughter understands what Jesus meant when He said, "My grace is sufficient for you, for My strength is made perfect in weakness."

2 CORINTHIANS 12:9

•

I pray that my daughter realizes that in all these things she is more than a conqueror through You who loved her.

ROMANS 8:37

•

I pray that whatever my daughter does she does it heartily, as to You, Lord, and not to men.

COLOSSIANS 3:23

1·1·2016

Granny? I came home from the
hospital last night. We were
exhausted.
All day today I've thought of you.
This situation you're in is heart
wrenching!"
I wasn't sure why you went with Izy?
You have to be stronger ... you brought
the New Year in at Billy Bobs?"
You're not of the world, I feel like
You desire things of the world though.
You are confused but you aren't diligently
seeking after Jesus! Why - you need
His wisdom? knowledge so bad.
Ryan asked me to Face time tonight, I'm
waiting on him.
I feel like your being motivated by
fear. You are so affraid of tribulation
All I know is that thru trial we
persevere - we grow especially
when we rely on God. Maybe

that's what's wrong — you aren't really relying
on Him or in Him.

I want to encourage you. I guess as a
mom I wish I could motivate you to
just TRUST GOD!

I'm excited I get to see you soon...
all I want to do is hug you. I miss
you so much and I love you even
more.

I read about King Solomon tonight. I
pondered on how he was unfaithful
to God. How his heart was led
astray from God.

We must put on the armor & ask
God for a hedge of protection.
If we fail Him we must confess
our sin and return to Him.
He is faithful! God is our strength &
strong tower.

CONDEMNED

Lord God, I ask You to keep in my daughter's mind at all times that there is no condemnation for those that are in Christ Jesus. Help her to know that if she trusts in Jesus she need not let Satan bring thoughts of doubt and condemnation to her mind. Thank You, Lord, for removing all such thoughts and feelings from my daughter. Thank You in Jesus' name. Amen.

God, in accordance
with Your Word . . .

I pray that my daughter will draw near with a true heart in full assurance of faith, having her heart sprinkled from an evil conscience and her body washed with pure water.

HEBREWS 10:22

———————— • ————————

I pray that my daughter always remembers that You, the LORD her God, are gracious and merciful, and will not turn Your face from her if she returns to You.

2 CHRONICLES 30:9

———●———

I pray that my daughter knows that it was You, God, who said that, "I, even I, am He who blots out your transgressions for My own sake."

ISAIAH 43:25

———●———

I pray that You did not send Your Son into the world to condemn my daughter, but that my daughter through Him might be saved. She who believes in Him is not condemned.

JOHN 3:17–18

———●———

I pray that my daughter, who hears Your word, Jesus, and believes in Him who sent You, has everlasting life, and shall not come into judgment, but has passed from death into life.

JOHN 5:24

I pray that You, God, will be merciful to my daughter's unrighteousness, and to her sins, and to her lawless deeds and that You remember them no more.

HEBREWS 8:12

———————— ● ————————

I pray that my daughter will forsake any wicked ways and any unrighteous thoughts. Let her return to You, LORD, and You will have mercy on her and abundantly pardon her.

ISAIAH 55:7

———————— ● ————————

I pray that my daughter will acknowledge her sin to You, God, and her iniquity she has not hidden. And that she will confess her transgressions to You so You can forgive the iniquity of her sins.

PSALM 32:5

I pray that if my daughter will confess her sins, You, God, are faithful and just to forgive her sins and to cleanse her from all unrighteousness.

1 JOHN 1:9

———————— ● ————————

I pray that there is therefore now no condemnation to my daughter who is in Christ Jesus, who does not walk according to the flesh, but according to the Spirit. For the law of the Spirit of life in Christ Jesus has made her free from the law of sin and death.

ROMANS 8:1–2

———————— ● ————————

I pray that as far as the east is from the west, so far have You removed my daughter's transgressions from her.

PSALM 103:12

I pray that if my daughter is in You, Christ, she is a new creation; old things have passed away; behold, all things have become new.

2 CORINTHIANS 5:17

———— ● ————

I pray that my daughter is blessed, whose transgression is forgiven, whose sin is covered.

PSALM 32:1

———— ● ————

I pray that my daughter has overcome Satan by the blood of the Lamb and by the word of her testimony.

REVELATION 12:11

———— ● ————

I pray that my daughter remembers that Jesus Himself said, "Neither do I condemn you; go and sin no more."

JOHN 8:11

I pray, God, that You will forgive my
daughter's iniquity, and her sin You will
remember no more.

JEREMIAH 31:34

Oh God You are so faithful!
Thank You for the promises and
the power in Your word — they last
forever!

God I pray for Ryan that he won't
condemn Catie. I pray that she
takes care of her business — that
she'll be lead by Your Spirit.
Thank You for the sweetness
of friends that loved on her
tonight. They are Your love
sent down to her.

Help her through this trial to
be set free. Remove the chains
that are binding. God may
she desire to please You thru
this trial.

1) That You would reveal Yourself to her. That she would strive to see Your face in and thru all of this.

2) For godly women to be raised up and brought into her life that pray for her and pour into her. That are willing to speak truth and love over her and will courageously call her out.

3) May she make You 1st, her everything, her 1st desire, her 1st thought, the one she runs to. May You be her 1st love

4) May You remove anyone or anything that is not Your will for her life. Remove those that aren't supposed to be near her and are not in Your plans for her.

4 *1.4.16*

CONFIDENCE

Lord Jesus, based upon God's word I call upon You to literally fill my daughter with confidence. Give her the spiritual confidence to know that whatever she asks in Your name she will receive. Fill her with the confidence that only You can give. Thank You for honoring Your word and my prayers. Amen.

God, in accordance
with Your Word . . .

I pray that when my daughter passes through the waters, You will be with her; and through the rivers, they shall not overflow her. When she walks through the fire, she shall not be burned, nor shall the flame scorch her.

ISAIAH 43:2

———— ● ————

I pray, God, that my daughter always re-members that it is You who justifies.

ROMANS 8:33

I pray that this is the confidence that my daughter has in You, Jesus, that if she asks anything according to Your will, You hear her. And if she knows that You hear her, whatever she asks, she knows that she has the petitions that she asked of You.

1 JOHN 5:14–15

●

I pray that when my daughter faces an obstacle she always remembers that God has said that it is "Not by might nor by power, but by My Spirit."

ZECHARIAH 4:6

●

I pray that whatever my daughter asks in Jesus' name, You will do it.

JOHN 14:14

●

I pray that You, the LORD God, are my daughter's strength.

HABAKKUK 3:19

I pray that my daughter will not cast away her confidence, which has great reward. For she has need of endurance, so that after she has done Your will, God, she may receive the promise.

HEBREWS 10:35–36

———— ● ————

I pray that my daughter will be confident of this very thing, that You who have begun a good work in her will complete it until the day of Jesus Christ.

PHILIPPIANS 1:6

———— ● ————

I pray that my daughter can do all things through Christ who strengthens her.

PHILIPPIANS 4:13

———— ● ————

I pray that my daughter may boldly say: 'The Lord is my helper; I will not fear. What can a person do to me?"

HEBREWS 13:6

I pray that if my daughter's heart does not condemn her, she will have confidence toward You, God.

1 JOHN 3:21

———— ● ————

I pray that if my daughter will wait on You, LORD, she shall renew her strength. She shall mount up with wings like eagles. She shall run and not be weary, she shall walk and not faint.

ISAIAH 40:31

1.4.16 ～

Oh God Your promises are so
incredible — Nothing is to hard
for You!
I have the confidence Lord —
I believe Your every word.
I ask that You would reveal
Yourself to Catherine — steady
her heart. Let her feel Your
presence each step of the way.
God I seek after You for her
future internship I trust You as
You take her thru this journey.
I pray Your perfect will over
this situation.

We praise that city & state
the Lord has
made before her
with the free, her
heart and living experience
Let her graduate &
this internship in Your
righteous right hand.
God You are in control
of her future and
are pleased by the
them there in placed
keep her in the town
the city.

CONFUSED

Heavenly Father, in the beautiful and precious name of Jesus, my Lord and my Savior, I ask You to remove all confusion from my daughter. Help her to know that Your word says You are the author of peace and not of confusion and that she is to lean on You and Your word and not her own understanding. Thank You in Jesus' name for honoring this prayer for my wonderful and precious daughter. Amen.

**God, in accordance
with Your Word . . .**

I pray that my daughter will trust in You, LORD, with all her heart, and lean not on her own understanding. I pray that in all her ways she will acknowledge You, and You will direct her paths.

PROVERBS 3:5–6

I pray that You, God, will instruct my daughter and teach her in the way she should go.

PSALM 32:8

———— ● ————

I pray that my daughter has great peace because she loves Your law, and nothing can cause her to stumble.

PSALM 119:165

———— ● ————

I pray that my daughter will always cast her burdens on You, LORD, and You shall sustain her.

PSALM 55:22

———— ● ————

I pray that my daughter will always remember that God gives power to the weak, and to those who have no might He increases strength.

ISAIAH 40:29

I pray that when my daughter passes through the waters, You will be with her. And when she passes through the rivers, they shall not overflow her. When she walks through the fire, she shall not be burned, nor shall the flame scorch her. For You are the LORD her God.

ISAIAH 43:2–3

●

I pray that my daughter will be anxious for nothing, but in everything by prayer and supplication, with thanksgiving, let her requests be made known to You, God, and Your peace, which surpasses all understanding, will guard her heart and mind through Christ Jesus.

PHILIPPIANS 4:6–7

●

I pray that when my daughter feels confused she will remember and understand that You, God, are not the author of confusion but of peace.

1 CORINTHIANS 14:33

I pray, God, that You have not given my daughter a spirit of fear, but of power and of love and of a sound mind.

2 TIMOTHY 1:7

———— ● ————

I pray that my daughter knows that where envy and self-seeking exist, confusion and every evil thing will be there. But the wisdom that is from above is first pure, then peaceable, gentle, willing to yield, full of mercy and good fruits, without partiality and without hypocrisy.

JAMES 3:16–17

———— ● ————

I pray that You, Lord God, will help my daughter; therefore she will not be disgraced.

ISAIAH 50:7

———— ● ————

I pray that my daughter will not think it strange concerning the fiery trial which is to try her, as though some strange thing

happened to her; but that she will rejoice
to the extent that she partakes of Christ's
sufferings, that when His glory is revealed,
she may also be glad with exceeding joy.

1 PETER 4:12–13

———— ● ————

I pray that if my daughter lacks wisdom, let
her ask of You, God, who gives to all liberally
and without reproach, and it will be given
to her.

JAMES 1:5

1.7.16

Lord God all I see is Your
goodness and Your mercy.
You have provided and
blessed Catie today as she
met with the woman @
the Veterans hospital. Thank
You Lord again & again!!
I'm lifting her up to You thru
this trial - You are our rock
and our fortress, our ever present
help in time of trouble!
Draw her near to You Lord.
Give her wisdom and discernment
Give her clarity and Confirmation
so she can choose. She has
just toiled in vain - reveal
Yourself to her, let her feel
Your presence, lift her up
in Your righteous right hand.
I ask You to remove all the
fear and confusion and

bitterness. Let her move foward
and not dwell in the past
in all that hurt and pain.
Let her see Ryan and Trey thru
Your eyes. Remind her they're
Your Sons.
She has been so dedicated to
social media and her flashy
way — bind up the enemy Lord
and remove him; We rebuke him.
Cast him out and don't allow
him to tempt her and ruin her.
May her desire to please You grow
great. May she walk with the
confidence and sure footing
because You provided it.
May she decrease so that You
can increase. You are, our
ever present help in this trouble
and trial. Lead us into Your
everlasting way. Amen!

COURAGE

Perfect God, grant my daughter the courage that only You can give. Help her to remember that You promised in Your word that she can do all things through Jesus and that she should never be afraid or discouraged or dismayed because You, her God, will be with her always. Thank You, God, in Jesus' name, for filling my daughter with courage. Amen.

God, in accordance with Your Word . . .

I pray that my daughter will never fear, for You, God, are with her. I pray that she will not be dismayed, for You are her God. I pray that You will strengthen her and help her and that You will uphold her with Your righteous right hand.

ISAIAH 41:10

I pray that my daughter will be persuaded
that neither death nor life, nor angels nor
principalities nor powers, nor things present
nor things to come, nor height nor depth,
nor any other created thing, shall be able
to separate her from the love of God which
is in Christ Jesus her Lord.

ROMANS 8:38–39

———— ● ————

I pray that my daughter shall not die, but
live, and declare the works of the LORD.

PSALM 118:17

———— ● ————

I pray that You, the eternal God, are my
daughter's refuge and that You will thrust
out the enemy from before her.

DEUTERONOMY 33:27

———— ● ————

I pray that my daughter can do all things
through Christ who strengthens her.

PHILIPPIANS 4:13

I pray that my daughter will wait on You,
LORD; that she will be of good courage, and
You shall strengthen her heart.

PSALM 27:14

———— ● ————

I pray that my daughter does not think it
strange concerning the fiery trial which is
to try her, as though some strange thing
happened to her; but that she will rejoice
to the extent that she partakes of Christ's
sufferings, that when His glory is revealed,
she may also be glad with exceeding joy.

1 PETER 4:12–13

———— ● ————

I pray that when my daughter passes through
the waters, You will be with her; and through
the rivers, they shall not overflow her. When
she walks through the fire, she shall not be
burned, nor shall the flame scorch her. For
You are the LORD her God.

ISAIAH 43:2–3

I pray that while my daughter's weeping may endure for a night, joy comes to her in the morning.

PSALM 30:5

---●---

I pray that my daughter will be of good courage and that You shall strengthen her heart, for her hope is in You, LORD.

PSALM 31:24

---●---

I pray that my daughter shall obtain joy and gladness and that sorrow and sighing shall flee away.

ISAIAH 51:11

---●---

I pray that my daughter will wait on You, LORD, and that she shall renew her strength. I pray that she shall mount up with wings like eagles; that she shall run and not be weary; that she shall walk and not faint.

ISAIAH 40:31

I pray that my daughter will be anxious for nothing, but in everything by prayer and supplication, with thanksgiving, will let her requests be made known to You, God.

PHILIPPIANS 4:6

I pray that whatever things are true, whatever things are noble, whatever things are just, whatever things are pure, whatever things are lovely, whatever things are of good report, if there is any virtue and if there is anything praiseworthy—that my daughter will meditate on these things.

PHILIPPIANS 4:8

1·8·16

Lord we rejoice as You
provide for Catie thru her
2 visits. We are so grateful
how You caused all things to
work together for her.
I am so thankful for Your
word and how I can pray for
her. Your word never comes
back void but accomplishes the
purpose You sent it out for.
May Catie stand and continue
to receive your wisdom. Open the
door and lead her in the
direction You would have
her to go. Help me Lord, teach
me to pray.
May he wait and worship as You
make all the provisions for her.
We worship You Lord - We bow
down and cry Holy!!

DELIVERANCE

Lord Jesus, today, at this very moment, I ask You to deliver my daughter from anything that is adversely afflicting her in any way. Help her to know the truth that comes only from You and Your word and to be set free from all that is upon her. Thank You, Jesus, for freeing my daughter and for filling her with joy and hope. Amen.

God, in accordance with Your Word . . .

I pray that my daughter shall know the truth, and the truth shall make her free.

JOHN 8:32

———————— ● ————————

I pray that if You, Jesus, make my daughter free, she shall be free indeed.

JOHN 8:36

I pray that there is therefore now no condemnation to my daughter who is in Christ Jesus, who does not walk according to the flesh, but according to the Spirit. For the law of the Spirit of life in Christ Jesus has made her free from the law of sin and death.

ROMANS 8:1–2

———— • ————

I pray that my daughter does not believe every spirit, but that she tests the spirits, whether they are of You, God; because many false prophets have gone out into the world. I pray that by this she will know the Spirit of God: that every spirit that confesses that Jesus Christ has come in the flesh is of God.

1 JOHN 4:1–2

———— • ————

I pray that He who is in my daughter is greater than he who is in the world.

1 JOHN 4:4

I pray that my daughter has overcome Satan
by the blood of the Lamb and by the word
of her testimony.

REVELATION 12:11

1·10·16

God thank You that Catherine
is with us!

1·30·16

God You are so faithful! You are
so generous to Your children!
Your word is a reminder of Your
commitment to us — It is the TRUTH
by which we should live our lives!
I know that Catie is in a deep
and desperate struggle — please
teach her to rely on You and to
seek after You. I am praying
that You would reveal
Yourself to her!
Bind up satan and cast him
out in the name of Jesus.
Whatever is lies in her life,
Whatever is not of You I pray
You expose it and reveal it
to her.

I don't know if Trey is who You want in her life. Help her to discern. Keep her heart true to You and steady for You. Keep them from falling into sexual sin. Convict her when her behavior isn't pleasing to You. Surround her with godly, fervent, passionate, humbled women who will invest in her and call her out in truth and love.

Help her as she works thru her feelings concerning Ryan.

Lord deliver her and use her for the furtherance of Your kingdom. Let her life be about Your will and not hers. May You transform her selfish desires to please You!

Carry her thru this day and may You shine Your face upon her day!

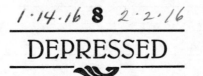

1·14·16 **8** *2·2·16*

DEPRESSED

Lord God, I pray to You now as always in Jesus' name. I ask You now in His name to remove any depression that may come upon my daughter at any time. Help her to know that if she will cry out to You that You will hear and deliver her. I pray Your word to You and I ask You to honor Your word and deliver her from any depression that she may ever experience. In Jesus' name, Amen.

God, in accordance
with Your Word . . .

I pray that my righteous daughter will cry out, and You will hear and deliver her out of all of her troubles.

PSALM 34:17

●

I pray that You are the God of my daughter's strength.

PSALM 43:2

I pray that while my daughter's weeping may endure for a night, her joy comes in the morning.

PSALM 30:5

———————— ● ————————

I pray that my daughter will wait on You, LORD. That she shall renew her strength. That she shall mount up with wings like eagles; that she shall run and not be weary and that she shall walk and not faint.

ISAIAH 40:31

———————— ● ————————

I pray, God, that You will comfort my daughter in all her tribulation, that she may be able to comfort those who are in any trouble, with the comfort with which she herself is comforted by You.

2 CORINTHIANS 1:4

———————— ● ————————

I pray that neither death nor life, nor angels nor principalities nor powers, nor things present nor things to come, nor height nor depth, nor any other created thing, shall be able to separate my daughter from Your love, God, which is in Christ Jesus her Lord.

ROMANS 8:38–39

———— ● ————

I pray that my daughter does not think it strange concerning the fiery trial which is to try her, as though some strange thing has happened to her; but that she will rejoice to the extent that she partakes of Christ's sufferings, so that when His glory is revealed, she may also be glad with exceeding joy.

1 PETER 4:12–13

———— ● ————

I pray that whatever things are true, whatever things are noble, whatever things are just, whatever things are pure, whatever things are lovely, whatever things are of good report, if there is any virtue and if there is anything praiseworthy—that my daughter will meditate on these things.

PHILIPPIANS 4:8

I pray, God, that You will heal my daughter's broken heart and bind up her wounds.

PSALM 147:3

———— ● ————

I pray that my daughter will fear not, for You are with her. That she will not be dismayed, for You are her God. I pray that You will strengthen her; that You will help her and that You will uphold her with Your righteous right hand.

ISAIAH 41:10

———— ● ————

I pray that my daughter will always pray and not lose heart.

LUKE 18:1

———— ● ————

I pray that my daughter will not sorrow, for the joy of the Lord is her strength.

NEHEMIAH 8:10

I pray that my daughter will humble herself under the mighty hand of God, that You may exalt her in due time. I pray that she will cast all her cares upon You, for You care for her.

1 PETER 5:6–7

2·2·16

Lord God You are our rescuer —
You are our deliverer. Praise
You for how You love us and
How we are victorious in You!
May Catie find peace tonight
in You and Your promises.
God give her great strength
as she battles flesh and it's
desires. Give her great courage
in the midst of this adversity!
I know the enemy wants her to feel
overwhelmed and overpowered
but Lord let her feel renewed
and let her mount up with
wings like an eagle and not be
weary or faint (Isaiah 40:31)
Bless her and make Your face
shine upon her. May Your
steadfast love be her guide and
shelter. I love You Lord —
I praise and worship You.

2·3·16 **9**

DESERTED BY LOVED ONES

Heavenly Father, I plead with You at this moment to honor Your word and set my daughter on high. Your word has promised that You will never leave her or forsake her, no matter what her loved ones might do. She needs You now. Draw her close to You and carry her burdens for her. In Your Son Jesus' name I pray. Amen.

God, in accordance
with Your Word . . .

I pray that because You have set Your love upon my daughter, therefore You will deliver her; You will set her on high, because she has known Your name. I pray that she shall call upon You, and You will answer her; You will be with her in trouble; You will deliver her and honor her. That with long life You will satisfy her, and show her Your salvation.

PSALM 91:14–16

I pray, God, that You will not forsake my
daughter nor destroy her.

DEUTERONOMY 4:31

———— ● ————

I pray that You, God, will hear my daughter
and that You will not forsake her.

ISAIAH 41:17

———— ● ————

I pray that my daughter will cast all her cares
upon You, God, for You care for her.

1 PETER 5:7

———— ● ————

I pray that even though my daughter is
hard pressed on every side, yet she is not
crushed; she is perplexed, but not in
despair; persecuted, but not forsaken; struck
down, but not destroyed—always carrying
about in her body the dying of the Lord
Jesus, that the life of Jesus also may be
manifested in her body.

2 CORINTHIANS 4:8–10

I pray that my daughter will no longer be
forsaken and You will delight in her.

ISAIAH 62:4

———————— ● ————————

I pray that because my daughter knows Your
name, God, she will put her trust in You;
for You, LORD, have not forsaken those who
seek You.

PSALM 9:10

———————— ● ————————

I pray that if even I forsake my daughter
that You will take care of her.

PSALM 27:10

———————— ● ————————

I pray that my daughter will be taught to
observe all things that Jesus has commanded
and that she knows that You are with her
always, even to the end of the age.

MATTHEW 28:20

I pray that my daughter always remembers
that You will not forget her.

ISAIAH 49:15

———————— ● ————————

I pray that my daughter's hope is in You,
God, and that she shall yet praise You, the
help of her countenance and her God.

PSALM 43:5

———————— ● ————————

I pray that my daughter will be strong and
of good courage. That she will not fear nor
be afraid; for You, the LORD her God, are the
One who goes with her. I know that You will
not leave her nor forsake her.

DEUTERONOMY 31:6

———————— ● ————————

I pray that You will not forsake my daughter,
for Your great name's sake, because it has
pleased You to make her one of Your people.

1 SAMUEL 12:22

2·3·16

Lord we rejoice in You tonight
because You hold Her in Your
righteous right hand.
God take her higher and remove
from her the dross. Prepare
her heart to receive Your
blessings.
Tomorrow as she fellowships
cause her heart to be burdened
w/ loving others as You do.
Use her in the groups she participates
in - cause her focus to be on
others and not herself.
Bless her time w/ her christian
friends.
Help Trey & Help Ryan - cause them
to be humbled and to seek after
You. Whatever You plan Lord let
us move our hearts & prayers
toward that - Let us be @ peace.
Let us not manipulate or try and

for a what is not Your will.

Give Catie the energy and what she needs to fill out her applications. Give her a clean mind.

Thank You Lord — You are our hope! We love you.

DISCOURAGED

Perfect God, in Jesus' name I ask You to remove
from my daughter any discouragement that she
may be feeling at this time in her life. Teach her
what Your word means when it says to wait on You,
and to be of good courage and that You, God, will
strengthen her. Thank You for hearing and honoring Your words. Amen.

God, in accordance
with Your Word . . .

I pray that my daughter will wait on You,
LORD; that she will be of good courage, and
that You will strengthen her heart.

PSALM 27:14

———————— ● ————————

I pray that my daughter will be of good
courage and that You, God, shall strengthen
her heart.

PSALM 31:24

I pray that my daughter shall obtain joy and gladness and that sorrow and sighing shall flee away.

ISAIAH 51:11

I pray that my daughter will not cast away her confidence, which has great reward. For she has need of endurance, so that after she has done Your will, God, she may receive her promise.

HEBREWS 10:35–36

I pray that my daughter is confident of this very thing, that You, God, who have begun a good work in her will complete it until the day of Jesus Christ.

PHILIPPIANS 1:6

I pray that my daughter does not grow weary while doing good, for in due season she shall reap if she does not lose heart.

GALATIANS 6:9

I pray that my daughter will greatly rejoice, though now for a little while, if need be, she may be grieved by various trials. I pray that the genuineness of her faith, being much more precious than gold that perishes, though it is tested by fire, may be found to praise, honor, and glory at the revelation of Jesus Christ, whom having not seen, she loves. Though now she does not see Him, yet believing, she rejoices with joy inexpressible and full of glory, receiving the end of her faith—the salvation of her soul.

1 PETER 1:6–9

●

I pray that my daughter will be anxious for nothing, but in everything by prayer and supplication, with thanksgiving, will let her request be made known to You, God; and Your peace, which surpasses all understanding, will guard her heart and mind through Christ Jesus.

PHILIPPIANS 4:6–7

I pray, God, that though my daughter walks in the midst of trouble, You will revive her. You will stretch out Your hand against the wrath of her enemies. I pray that with Your right hand You will save her.

PSALM 138:7

———— ● ————

I pray that my daughter will not let her heart be troubled. That she will believe in You, God, and also in Jesus.

JOHN 14:1

———— ● ————

I pray that even though my daughter is hard pressed on every side, she is not crushed; she is perplexed, but not in despair; persecuted, but not forsaken; struck down, but not destroyed—always carrying about in her body the dying of the Lord Jesus, that the life of Jesus also may be manifested in her body.

2 CORINTHIANS 4:8–10

2.6.16

Lord God You are so good! all
of Your scripture is truth
and Your word is powerful!
I stand on Your truth tonight
as Catie & Ryan talk.
Oh God help them die to their
flesh and to open their heart
so that Your Spirit may
minister to them.
"Blessed is the man who makes the
Lord his trust." Psalm 40:4

My heart is so heavy and ...
teach me Your way. Help
me to be faithful. Keep me
focused.

DISSATISFIED

Lord Jesus, through the power of Your perfect and error-free word I call upon You to replace any dissatisfaction in my daughter's life with joy, hope, and happiness. Your word says her soul will be satisfied and she shall have every good thing. Through my faith and the authority of Your word I now ask that You hear and honor these words from the Bible. Thank You for hearing my prayers. Amen.

God, in accordance
with Your Word . . .

I pray that my daughter can do all things
through Christ who strengthens her.

PHILIPPIANS 4:13

●

I pray that my daughter will be satisfied
with good by the fruit of her mouth.

PROVERBS 12:14

I pray that my daughter's soul shall be
satisfied as with marrow and fatness, and
her mouth shall praise You with joyful lips.

PSALM 63:5

———— ● ————

I pray that my daughter will bless You, LORD,
with all that is within her and that she will
forget not all Your benefits. I pray that she
will not forget who forgives all her iniquities
and who heals all her diseases. I pray that
she will not forget who redeems her life
from destruction and who crowns her with
lovingkindness and tender mercies and
who satisfies her mouth with good things,
so that her youth is renewed like the eagle's.

PSALM 103:1–5

———— ● ————

I pray, God, that You will satisfy my
daughter's longing soul, and fill her
hungry soul with goodness.

PSALM 107:9

I pray that because my daughter seeks You, LORD, she shall not lack any good thing.

PSALM 34:10

———————— ● ————————

I pray that my daughter will delight herself in You, LORD, and You shall give her the desires of her heart.

PSALM 37:4

———————— ● ————————

I pray that my daughter will trust and not be afraid; for You, God, are her strength and her song. You have become her salvation.

ISAIAH 12:2

———————— ● ————————

I pray that You, God, who supplies seed to the sower and bread for food, will supply and multiply the seed my daughter has sown and increase the fruits of her righteousness.

2 CORINTHIANS 9:10

2·/8·/6

DISTRESS / SADNESS

God in heaven, You have promised the comfort of the Holy Spirit to us in times such as this. I ask You for a special comforting for my daughter. Your word says that while sadness may come upon her that her joy will return in the morning. I pray this, Your word, for my daughter. Remove her distress. Take away her sadness. And honor these Your words that I am about to pray. Thank You in Jesus' name. Amen.

God, in accordance with Your Word . . .

I pray that my daughter has done justice and righteousness and that You will not leave her to her oppressors.

PSALM 119:121

I pray that You, God, will strengthen my daughter according to Your word.

PSALM 119:28

I pray that while my daughter may be despised, she does not forget Your precepts.

PSALM 119:141

———— ● ————

I pray that while trouble and anguish have overtaken my daughter, Your commandments are her delights. The righteousness of Your testimonies is everlasting. I pray that You will give her understanding, and she shall live.

PSALM 119:143–144

———— ● ————

It is good for my daughter that she has been afflicted so that she may learn from Your statutes.

PSALM 119:71

———— ● ————

I pray that You, God, will consider my daughter's affliction and deliver her, for she does not forget Your law. I pray that

You will plead her cause and redeem her.
Revive her according to Your word.

PSALM 119:153–154

———————— ● ————————

I pray that in righteousness my daughter
shall be established. That she shall be far
from oppression, for she shall not fear;
and from terror, for it shall not come near
her.

ISAIAH 54:14

———————— ● ————————

I pray that my daughter has great peace
because she loves Your law, God, and
nothing causes her to stumble.

PSALM 119:165

———————— ● ————————

I pray that if my daughter has gone astray
like a lost sheep, that You, God, will seek
her, Your servant, and not let her forget
Your commandments.

PSALM 119:176

I pray that my daughter will always pray,
"Blessed be the Lord," who daily loads her
with benefits.

PSALM 68:19

———— ● ————

I pray, God, that You will bring my
daughter up out of a horrible pit and out
of the miry clay. Set her feet upon a rock
and establish her steps.

PSALM 40:2

———— ● ————

I pray that You, God, are my daughter's
refuge and strength, a very present help in
trouble and that she will not fear.

PSALM 46:1–2

———— ● ————

I pray that since Your name LORD is a strong
tower, that my righteous daughter runs to
it and is safe.

PROVERBS 18:10

I pray that my daughter will not let her
heart be troubled and that she will always
believe in God and in Jesus.

JOHN 14:1

———— ● ————

I pray that my daughter will not sorrow,
for the joy of the Lord is her strength.

NEHEMIAH 8:10

———— ● ————

I pray that my daughter will always live
with the realization that her Lord is faithful
and will establish her and guard her from
the evil one.

2 THESSALONIANS 3:3

DON'T UNDERSTAND GOD

Lord God, the words that I am about to pray are Your words. Hear them please and honor them. Help my daughter to understand that because Your thoughts are often higher than her thoughts that she may not always understand Your thoughts and Your way. Remind her of Your promise that if she will call upon You, You will tell her great and unsearchable things that she does not know. I pray Your word to You in Jesus' name. Amen.

God, in accordance with Your Word . . .

I pray that You, God, will help my daughter to understand that Your thoughts are not her thoughts, nor are her ways Your ways. That she will understand that as the heavens are higher than the earth, so are Your ways higher than her ways, and Your thoughts higher than her thoughts.

ISAIAH 55:8–9

I pray that my daughter will call to You,
God, and that You will answer her and show
her great and mighty things, which she
does not know.

JEREMIAH 33:3

———— ● ————

I pray that if You, God, are for my daughter,
who can be against her?

ROMANS 8:31

———— ● ————

I pray that in all things my daughter is more
than a conqueror through Him who loved
her.

ROMANS 8:37

———— ● ————

I pray that as for You, God, Your way is
perfect. The word of the LORD is proven;
You are a shield to my daughter who trusts
in You.

PSALM 18:30

I pray that my daughter will pursue the
knowledge of the LORD.

HOSEA 6:3

———— ● ————

I pray, God, that You will perfect that which
concerns my daughter and that Your mercy,
O LORD, endures forever.

PSALM 138:8

———— ● ————

I pray that You, God, will make an
everlasting covenant with my daughter,
that You will not turn away from doing her
good; but that You will put Your fear in her
heart so that she will not depart from You.

JEREMIAH 32:40

———— ● ————

I pray that my daughter will hold fast the
confession of her hope without wavering,
for You, God, who promised are faithful.

HEBREWS 10:23

I pray that all things work together for good
to my daughter who loves You, God, to
her who is the called according to Your
purpose.

ROMANS 8:28

●

I pray that no temptation has overtaken
my daughter except such as is common to
man; but You, God, are faithful, who
will not allow her to be tempted beyond
what she is able, but with the temptation
You will also make the way of escape, that
she may be able to bear it.

1 CORINTHIANS 10:13

●

I pray that my daughter will fear not, for
You, God, are with her. That she will be
not dismayed, for You are her God. That
You will strengthen her and help her. That
You will uphold her with Your righteous
right hand.

ISAIAH 41:10

I pray that my daughter will cast her burden
on You, LORD, and You shall sustain her.

PSALM 55:22

———————— ● ————————

I pray that while many are the afflictions of
my righteous daughter, You, LORD, deliver
her out of them all.

PSALM 34:19

———————— ● ————————

I pray that my daughter does not think it
strange concerning the fiery trial which is
to try her, as though some strange thing
happened; but that she will rejoice to the
extent that she partakes of Christ's
sufferings, that when His glory is revealed,
she may also be glad with exceeding joy.

1 PETER 4:12–13

DOUBTING GOD

Heavenly Father, today I pray the power of Your perfect word to remove any doubts about You that my daughter might have. Your word says that Your way is perfect and Your word is proven. Use Your Holy Spirit to impart Your perfection to my daughter and to remove any doubts that she may have now or at any time in her life. Help her more than ever before to believe and not doubt. And it is in Jesus' name that I pray. Amen.

God, in accordance with Your Word . . .

I pray that You, Lord, are not slack concerning Your promise, as some count slackness, but are longsuffering toward my daughter, not willing that she should perish but that she should come to repentance.

2 PETER 3:9

I pray that because Your way is perfect and Your word is proven; that You, God, are a shield to all who trust in You.

PSALM 18:30

———— ● ————

I pray that my daughter will always remember that Your hand is not shortened so that it cannot save; nor Your ear heavy, that it cannot hear.

ISAIAH 59:1

———— ● ————

I pray that my daughter knows that He who calls her is faithful, who also will do it.

1 THESSALONIANS 5:24

———— ● ————

I pray that my daughter does not seek what she should eat or what she should drink, nor have an anxious mind. For all these things the nations of the world seek after, and You, her Father, know that she needs these things. I pray that she will seek the kingdom of God, and all these things shall be added to her.

LUKE 12:29–31

———— ● ————

I pray, God, that my daughter is aware that You have said Your counsel shall stand, and You will do all Your pleasure. Indeed, You have spoken it and You will also bring it to pass. You have purposed it and You will also do it.

ISAIAH 46:10–11

———— ● ————

I pray that my daughter will always remember that You, God, have declared that, "So shall My word be that goes forth from My mouth; it shall not return to Me void, but it shall accomplish what I please, and it shall prosper in the thing for which I sent it."

ISAIAH 55:11

I pray that whatever things my daughter asks when she prays, that she will believe that she will receive them, and she will have them.

MARK 11:24

———————— ● ————————

I pray that my daughter knows that faith comes by hearing, and hearing by the word of God.

ROMANS 10:17

———————— ● ————————

I pray that my daughter does not think it strange concerning the fiery trial which is to try her, as though some strange thing happened. But that she rejoices to the extent that she partakes of Christ's sufferings, that when His glory is revealed, she may also be glad with exceeding joy.

1 PETER 4:12–13

2·21·16

EMOTIONALLY UPSET

Jesus, I am here to pray Your word and to ask You to give great peace to my daughter because she loves You so much. As Your word says, give her a sound mind and a peace that passes all under-standing. In accordance with Your word let her be anxious for nothing. Thank You, Jesus, for honor-ing Your word in this important time in my daugh-ter's life. Amen.

God, in accordance with Your Word . . .

I pray that my daughter will have great peace because she loves Your law, and nothing causes her to stumble.

PSALM 119:165

———— ● ————

I pray that You, God, will heal my daughter's broken heart and bind up her wounds.

PSALM 147:3

I pray that because my daughter believes in You, God, she will by no means be put to shame.

1 PETER 2:6

———— ● ————

I pray that You, God, will help my daughter; therefore she will not be disgraced. She can set her face like a flint and know that she will not be ashamed.

ISAIAH 50:7

———— ● ————

I pray that my daughter will cast her burden on You, LORD, and that You shall sustain her.

PSALM 55:22

———— ● ————

I pray that my daughter will be anxious for nothing, but in everything by prayer and supplication, with thanksgiving, will let her requests be made known to You, God; and Your peace, God, which surpasses all

understanding, will guard her heart and
mind through Christ Jesus.

PHILIPPIANS 4:6–7

———————— ● ————————

I pray that You, God, have not given my
daughter a spirit of fear, but of power and
of love and of a sound mind.

2 TIMOTHY 1:7

———————— ● ————————

I pray that my daughter will fear not, for
You, God, are with her. That she be not
dismayed, for You are her God. I pray that
You will strengthen her and help her and
that You will uphold her with Your
righteous right hand.

ISAIAH 41:10

———————— ● ————————

I pray that my daughter will realize that
You, God, are not the author of confusion
but of peace.

1 CORINTHIANS 14:33

I pray that my daughter knows that where envy and self-seeking exist, confusion and every evil thing will be there. I pray that she will also know that the wisdom that is from above is first pure, then peaceable, gentle, willing to yield, full of mercy and good fruits, without partiality and without hypocrisy and that the fruit of righteousness is sown in peace by those who make peace.

JAMES 3:16–18

———— ● ————

I pray that while my daughter's weeping may endure for a night, her joy comes in the morning.

PSALM 30:5

———— ● ————

I pray that when my daughter passes through the waters, You, God, will be with her. And when she passes through the rivers, they shall not overflow her. I pray that when she walks through the fire, she shall not be burned, nor shall the flame scorch her. You are the LORD her God.

ISAIAH 43:2–3

I pray that You, God, will comfort my daughter in all her tribulation, that she may be able to comfort those who are in any trouble, with the comfort with which she herself is comforted by You.

2 CORINTHIANS 1:4

———— ● ————

I pray that whatever things are true, whatever things are noble, whatever things are just, whatever things are pure, whatever things are lovely, whatever things are of good report, if there is any virtue and if there is anything praiseworthy—that my daughter will meditate on these things.

PHILIPPIANS 4:8

———— ● ————

I pray that neither death nor life, nor angels nor principalities nor powers, nor things present nor things to come, nor height nor depth, nor any other created thing, shall be able to separate my daughter from the love of God which is in Christ Jesus, her Lord.

ROMANS 8:38–39

2·21·16

Lord I ached in my heart but You
brought relief and peace !!
        Hallelujah to the King
    who saves and rescues.
Make it so evident to Catie
that You love her. May
    she feel Your very presence
now!

FAITH

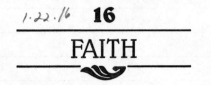

Father God, in the name of Your Son, Jesus, I pray to You Your perfect word for my daughter. Increase her faith. Help her to remember that You said she is to walk by faith and not by sight. Hear and answer Your word now concerning my daughter's faith. Thank You in Jesus' name. Amen.

God, in accordance with Your Word . . .

I pray that You, Lord, will increase my daughter's faith.

LUKE 17:5

———————— ● ————————

I pray that my daughter's faith comes by hearing, and hearing by the word of God.

ROMANS 10:17

I pray that my daughter will walk by faith
and not by sight.

2 CORINTHIANS 5:7

———— ● ————

I pray that my daughter will have a pure
heart, a good conscience, and sincere faith.

1 TIMOTHY 1:5

———— ● ————

I pray that my daughter will always
remember that faith is the substance of
things hoped for and the evidence of
things not seen.

HEBREWS 11:1

———— ● ————

I pray that my daughter remembers that
faith by itself, if it does not have works, is
dead.

JAMES 2:17

I pray that my daughter will constantly take the shield of faith with which she will be able to quench all the fiery darts of the wicked one.

EPHESIANS 6:16

———— ● ————

I pray that my daughter will put on the breastplate of faith and love, and as her helmet the hope of salvation.

1 THESSALONIANS 5:8

———— ● ————

I pray that my daughter will always have faith and a good conscience.

1 TIMOTHY 1:19

———— ● ————

I pray that my daughter will draw near with a true heart in full assurance of faith and that she will have her heart sprinkled from an evil conscience and her body washed with pure water.

HEBREWS 10:22

I pray that my daughter will fight the good fight of faith, that she will lay hold on eternal life, to which she was also called.

1 TIMOTHY 6:12

I pray that my daughter understands that without faith it is impossible to please You, God, and that for her to come to You she must believe that You are and that You are a rewarder of those who diligently seek You.

HEBREWS 11:6

I pray that my daughter will be just and will live by faith.

HABAKKUK 2:4

I pray that my daughter will remember that Abraham believed God, and it was accounted to him for righteousness.

ROMANS 4:3

I pray that my daughter, having been justified by faith, will have peace with You, God, through her Lord Jesus Christ.

ROMANS 5:1

———— ● ————

I pray that my daughter will count all things as a loss for the excellence of the knowledge of Christ Jesus, her Lord, for whom she has suffered the loss of all things, and count them as rubbish, that she may gain Christ and be found in Him, not having her own righteousness, which is from the law, but that which is through faith in Christ, the righteousness which is from God by faith; that she may know Him and the power of His resurrection, and the fellowship of His sufferings, being conformed to His death.

PHILIPPIANS 3:8–10

———— ● ————

I pray that my daughter will be just and will live by faith.

HEBREWS 10:38

I pray that my daughter shall believe in
You, the LORD her God, and that she shall
be established. I pray also that she will
believe Your prophets and she shall prosper.

2 CHRONICLES 20:20

———— ● ————

I pray that according to my daughter's
faith, it will be to her.

MATTHEW 9:29

———— ● ————

I pray that my daughter will have faith as a
mustard seed and she will say to her
mountain, "Move from here to there," and
it will move; and nothing will be
impossible for her.

MATTHEW 17:20

———— ● ————

I pray that my daughter will have faith in
You, God.

MARK 11:22

I pray for my daughter the righteousness
of You, God, which is through faith in
Jesus Christ on her who believes.

ROMANS 3:22

———— ● ————

I pray, God, that in Your forbearance You
have passed over my daughter's sins that
were previously committed.

ROMANS 3:25

———— ● ————

I pray that my daughter will remember
that if she has the gift of prophecy, and
understands all mysteries and all
knowledge, and though she has all faith, so
that she can remove mountains, but has
not love, she is nothing.

1 CORINTHIANS 13:2

———— ● ————

I pray that my daughter will watch and
that she will stand fast in the faith and that
she will be brave and strong.

1 CORINTHIANS 16:13

I pray that my daughter will examine herself as to whether she is in the faith and that she will test herself.

2 CORINTHIANS 13:5

———— ● ————

I pray that my daughter knows that she is not justified by the works of the law but by faith in Jesus Christ.

GALATIANS 2:16

———— ● ————

I pray that my daughter has been crucified with Christ. That it is no longer she who lives, but Christ who lives in her. And that the life which she now lives in the flesh she lives by faith in the Son of God, who loves her and gave Himself for her.

GALATIANS 2:20

———— ● ————

I pray that my daughter understands that as the body without the spirit is dead, so faith without works is dead also.

JAMES 2:26

I pray that my daughter knows the Holy Scriptures, which are able to make her wise for salvation through her faith which is in Christ Jesus.

2 TIMOTHY 3:15

———— ● ————

I pray that my daughter will fight the good fight; that she will finish the race; and that she will keep the faith.

2 TIMOTHY 4:7

———— ● ————

I pray that the sharing of my daughter's faith may become effective by the acknowledgment of every good thing which is in her in Christ Jesus.

PHILEMON 1:6

———— ● ————

I pray that my daughter will realize that if she does not believe she shall not be established.

ISAIAH 7:9

I pray that it is by faith that my daughter understands that the worlds were framed by the word of God, so that the things which are seen were not made of things which are visible.

HEBREWS 11:3

———— ● ————

I pray that my daughter will always look unto Jesus, the author and finisher of her faith, who for the joy that was set before Him endured the cross, despising the shame, and has sat down at the right hand of the throne of God.

HEBREWS 12:2

FEAR

God, I pray Your word to You now to remove any and all fears that my daughter may be harboring either now or in the future. I ask You to remember that my prayers are actually Your words on the subject of fear. Please honor Your perfect and error-free word and remove any and all fears now and forever in my daughter. Thank You, God, for hearing my prayers. In Jesus' name. Amen.

God, in accordance with Your Word . . .

I pray that Your truth, God, shall be my daughter's shield and buckler and that she shall not be afraid.

PSALM 91:4–5

●

I pray that no evil shall befall my daughter.

PSALM 91:10

I pray that my daughter will not be afraid of sudden terror, nor of trouble from the wicked when it comes. I pray that You, LORD, will be her confidence and will keep her foot from being caught.

PROVERBS 3:25–26

———— ● ————

I pray that in righteousness my daughter shall be established. She shall be far from oppression, for she shall not fear. And from terror, for it shall not come near her.

ISAIAH 54:14

———— ● ————

I pray that in You, God, my daughter will put her trust and that she will not be afraid.

PSALM 56:11

———— ● ————

I pray that my daughter knows that You, God, have not given her a spirit of fear, but of power and of love and of a sound mind.

2 TIMOTHY 1:7

I pray that my daughter did not receive
the spirit of bondage again to fear, but that
she received the Spirit of adoption by
whom she cries out, "Abba, Father."

ROMANS 8:15

———— ● ————

I pray that in my daughter there is no fear
in love; because perfect love casts out fear.

1 JOHN 4:18

———— ● ————

I pray that You, God, will give Your angels
charge over my daughter, to keep her in
all her ways.

PSALM 91:11

———— ● ————

I pray that though my daughter walks
through the valley of the shadow of death,
she will fear no evil; for You, God, are with
her. Your rod and Your staff, they comfort
her.

PSALM 23:4

I pray that my daughter will be of good courage and that You, God, shall strengthen her heart, for her hope is in the LORD.

PSALM 31:24

———— ● ————

I pray that my daughter receives the peace that You, Jesus, have left with her, the peace You gave to her. Let not her heart be troubled, neither let it be afraid.

JOHN 14:27

———— ● ————

I pray that You, LORD, are my daughter's light and her salvation. Whom shall she fear? Though an army may encamp against her, her heart shall not fear. In this she will be confident.

PSALM 27:1, 3

———— ● ————

I pray that You, Lord, are my daughter's helper and that she will not fear.

HEBREWS 13:6

I pray that if You, God, are for my daughter, who can be against her? Who shall separate her from the love of Christ? Shall tribulation, or distress, or persecution, or famine, or nakedness, or peril, or sword? I pray that in all these things she is more than a conqueror through Him who loved her. For I am persuaded that neither death nor life, nor angels nor principalities nor powers, nor things present nor things to come, nor height nor depth, nor any other created thing, shall be able to separate my daughter from Your love, God, which is in Christ Jesus her Lord.

ROMANS 8:31, 35, 37–39

2.23.16

Hallelujah to You God! You
are our Rock and our
Hiding Place our ever present
help in time of trouble.
You have answered our
pray and we thank You!
We have been tremendously blessed!

2·24·16 **18**

FINANCIAL PROBLEMS

Heavenly Father, it is not Your will that my daughter should have to contend unnecessarily with financial problems. Because I believe strongly in Your word, I present to You as my prayers for my daughter Your very words on this subject. Please honor Your word and release her from any and all financial problems in her life. I pray Your words in Jesus' name. Amen.

God, in accordance with Your Word . . .

I pray that my daughter may prosper in all things and be in health, just as her soul prospers.

3 JOHN 1:2

———— ● ————

I pray that You, Lord, are my daughter's shepherd and that she shall not want.

PSALM 23:1

I pray that my daughter will seek You, Lord, and not lack any good thing.

PSALM 34:10

———— ● ————

I pray that all these blessings shall come upon my daughter and overtake her, because she obeys the voice of the Lord her God. She shall be blessed in the city and she shall be blessed in the country. She shall be blessed when she comes in and she shall be blessed when she goes out. I pray that You, Lord, will command Your blessing on her in her storehouses and in all to which she sets her hand.

DEUTERONOMY 28:2–3, 6, 8

———— ● ————

I pray that my daughter will give, and it will be given to her: good measure, pressed down, shaken together, and running over will be put into her bosom. For with the same measure that she uses, it will be measured back to her.

LUKE 6:38

I pray that because freely my daughter has received, freely she will give.

MATTHEW 10:8

———— ● ————

I pray that on the first day of the week my daughter will lay something aside, storing up as she may prosper, so that there be no collections when it is time to give.

1 CORINTHIANS 16:2

———— ● ————

I pray that my daughter will bring all her tithes into the storehouse, that there may be food in God's house. And that she will try You, God, in this and see if You will not open for her the windows of heaven and pour out for her such blessing that there will not be room enough to receive it.

MALACHI 3:10

———— ● ————

I pray that my daughter realizes that if she sows sparingly she will also reap sparingly, and if she sows bountifully she will also reap bountifully. I pray that she will give as she purposes in her heart, not grudgingly or of necessity; for You, God, love a cheerful giver. And You are able to make all grace abound toward her, that my daughter, always having all sufficiency in all things, may have an abundance for every good work.

2 CORINTHIANS 9:6–8

———————— ● ————————

I pray that my daughter will remember that everyone who has left houses or brothers or sisters or father or mother or daughter or children or lands, for Your name's sake, Lord, shall receive a hundredfold, and inherit eternal life. I pray also that she will remember that many who are first will be last, and the last first.

MATTHEW 19:29–30

———————— ● ————————

I pray that this Book of the Law shall not depart from my daughter's mouth, but she shall meditate in it day and night, that she may observe to do according to all that is written in it. For then she will make her way prosperous, and then she will have good success.

JOSHUA 1:8

———————— ● ————————

I pray, God, that You will give wisdom and knowledge and joy to my daughter who is good in Your sight; but to the sinner You will give the work of gathering and collecting, that he may give to my daughter who is good before You.

ECCLESIASTES 2:26

———————— ● ————————

I pray that my daughter leaves an inheritance to her children's children.

PROVERBS 13:22

———————— ● ————————

I pray that my daughter does not worry about her life, saying, "What shall I eat?" or

"What shall I drink?" or "What shall I put on?" For You, her Heavenly Father, know that she needs all these things. But I pray that she will seek first Your kingdom, God, and Your righteousness, and all these things shall be added to her. I also pray that she does not worry about tomorrow, for tomorrow will worry about its own things.

MATTHEW 6:25, 33–34

———— ● ————

I pray that You, God, shall supply all my daughter's needs according to Your riches in glory by Christ Jesus.

PHILIPPIANS 4:19

2.24.16

God it's not by happenstance that
these prayers came to be at
this time. Thank You for giving
me these promises to cling to.

19

FORGIVENESS

Lord God, for reasons known to You, my daughter needs Your forgiveness. Because I sense that and know that she has need of Your forgiveness I come to You today, praying that she might be forgiven. Bless now the very words from Your mouth on my daughter's behalf. Thank You now in Jesus' name. Amen.

God, in accordance
with Your Word . . .

I pray that as far as the east is from the west, so far have You, God, removed my daughter's transgressions from her.

PSALM 103:12

———— ● ————

I pray that my daughter's transgressions are forgiven and her sin is covered.

PSALM 32:1

I pray that in You, Jesus, my daughter has redemption through Your blood, the forgiveness of her sins, according to the riches of God's grace which He made to abound toward her in all wisdom and prudence, having made known to her the mystery of His will, according to His good pleasure which He purposed in Himself.

EPHESIANS 1:7–9

I pray that it is You who blots out my daughter's transgressions for Your own sake and that You will not remember her sins.

ISAIAH 43:25

I pray that my daughter will return to You, LORD, and that You will have mercy on her; and to her God, for You will abundantly pardon.

ISAIAH 55:7

I pray that You, God, will cleanse my
daughter from all her iniquity by which
she has sinned against You, and that You
will pardon all her iniquities by which she
has sinned and by which she has
transgressed against You.

JEREMIAH 33:8

———— ● ————

I pray that whenever my daughter stands
praying, if she has anything against anyone
that she will forgive them, so that You, her
Father in heaven, may also forgive her of
her trespasses.

MARK 11:25

———— ● ————

I pray that my daughter will bear with
others, and forgive others, if she has a
complaint against any others; even as
Christ forgave her, so she also must do.

COLOSSIANS 3:13

I pray that my daughter will walk by faith
and not by sight.

2 CORINTHIANS 5:7

———— ● ————

I pray that if my daughter confesses her
sins, that You, God, are faithful and just to
forgive her sins and to cleanse her from all
unrighteousness.

1 JOHN 1:9

———— ● ————

I pray that if my daughter sins, she has an
Advocate with You, the Father, Jesus Christ
the righteous.

1 JOHN 2:1

20
GODLY LIFE

Lord Jesus, my Lord and my Savior, more than
anything else I desire that my wonderful daughter
will live a godly life in Your sight. Your words are
my prayers to You on her behalf. Please honor
them by keeping my daughter in the center of Your
will in all that she does. Thank You for all that You
do and especially for honoring this my prayer.
Amen.

God, in accordance
with Your Word . . .

I pray that if my daughter lives, she lives to
You, Lord; and if she dies, she dies to You,
Lord. Therefore, whether she lives or dies,
she is Yours, Lord.

ROMANS 14:8

———— ● ————

I pray that what the law could not do in
my daughter because it was weak through
the flesh, You, God, did by sending Your

own Son in the likeness of sinful flesh, on account of sin: You condemned sin in my daughter, that the righteous requirement of the law might be fulfilled in her because she does not walk according to the flesh but according to the Spirit.

ROMANS 8:3–4

———— ● ————

I pray that my daughter does not present her members as instruments of unrighteousness to sin, but presents herself to You, God, as being alive from the dead, and her members as instruments of righteousness to You. For sin shall not have dominion over her, for she is not under law but under grace.

ROMANS 6:13–14

———— ● ————

I pray that my daughter will present her body as a living sacrifice, holy, acceptable to You, God.

ROMANS 12:1

I pray that if my daughter believes on You, Jesus, who justifies the ungodly, her faith is accounted for righteousness.

ROMANS 4:5

———— ● ————

I pray that my daughter will not think of herself more highly than she ought to think, but will think soberly, as You, God, have dealt to her a measure of faith.

ROMANS 12:3

———— ● ————

I pray that because You, Christ, are in my daughter, her body is dead because of sin, but the Spirit is life because of righteousness.

ROMANS 8:10

———— ● ————

I pray that my daughter whom You, God, predestined, You also called; whom You called, You also justified; and whom You justified, You also glorified.

ROMANS 8:30

I pray that my daughter will not be conformed to this world, but that she will be transformed by the renewing of her mind, that she may prove what is that good and acceptable and perfect will of God.

ROMANS 12:2

———— ● ————

I pray that because my daughter is in You, Christ, she is a new creation; old things have passed away; behold, all things have become new.

2 CORINTHIANS 5:17

———— ● ————

I pray that my daughter will remain in the same calling in which she was called.

1 CORINTHIANS 7:20

———— ● ————

I pray that if my daughter glories, she will glory in You, Lord.

1 CORINTHIANS 1:31

I pray that You, God, made Jesus who knew
no sin to be sin for my daughter, that she
might become the righteousness of You
in Him.

2 CORINTHIANS 5:21

●

I pray that You, God, are able to make all
grace abound toward my daughter, that
she, always having all sufficiency in all
things, may have an abundance for every
good work.

2 CORINTHIANS 9:8

●

I pray that my daughter will not let sin
reign in her mortal body, that she should
obey it in its lusts.

ROMANS 6:12

●

I pray that my daughter has been set free
from sin and has become a slave of God.

ROMANS 6:22

I pray that my daughter will be renewed in
the spirit of her mind, and that she will put
on her new self which was created
according to You, God, in true
righteousness and holiness.

EPHESIANS 4:23–24

———————— ● ————————

I pray that it is good for my daughter to
draw near to You, God; to put her trust in
the Lord God, that she may declare all
Your works.

PSALM 73:28

———————— ● ————————

I pray that my daughter will delight herself
in You, LORD, and that You shall give her
the desires of her heart.

PSALM 37:4

———————— ● ————————

I pray that You, God, will satisfy my
daughter's mouth with good things, so that
her youth is renewed like the eagle's.

PSALM 103:5

I pray that You, God, are a companion to my daughter who fears You and who keeps Your precepts.

PSALM 119:63

———— ● ————

I pray that my daughter, who walks in the law of the LORD will be blessed.

PSALM 119:1

———— ● ————

I pray that my daughter will cleanse her way by taking heed according to Your word, God.

PSALM 119:9

———— ● ————

I pray that with my daughter's whole heart she has sought You, God. Let her not wander from Your commandments.

PSALM 119:10

I pray that my daughter's ways are directed
to keep Your statutes, God.

PSALM 119:5

———————— ● ————————

I pray that my daughter has hidden Your
word in her heart, God, that she might not
sin against You.

PSALM 119:11

———————— ● ————————

I pray that my daughter will delight herself
in Your statutes, God, and that she will not
forget Your word.

PSALM 119:16

———————— ● ————————

I pray that my daughter has chosen the
way of truth and that Your judgments she
has laid before her. I pray that she will
cling to Your testimonies, LORD, and that
she will not be put to shame.

PSALM 119:30–31

I pray that You, God, will open my daughter's eyes, that she may see wondrous things from Your law.

PSALM 119:18

———— ● ————

I pray, God, that Your testimonies also are my daughter's delight and her counselors.

PSALM 119:24

———— ● ————

I pray that my daughter has declared her ways and that You, God, have answered her and that You will teach her Your statutes.

PSALM 119:26

———— ● ————

I pray that You, God, will make my daughter understand the way of Your precepts; so shall she meditate on Your wondrous works.

PSALM 119:27

I pray, God, that You will make my daughter
walk in the path of Your commandments
and that she will delight in it.

PSALM 119:35

I pray that my daughter will incline her
heart to Your testimonies, God, and not to
covetousness. I pray that she will turn
away her eyes from looking at worthless
things and that You will revive her in Your
way.

PSALM 119:36-37

I pray that You, God, will remember the
word to my daughter, Your servant, upon
which You have caused her to hope.

PSALM 119:49

I pray that You, God, will be merciful to
my daughter according to Your word.

PSALM 119:58

I pray, O God, that my daughter has
thought about her ways, and has turned
her feet to Your testimonies. I pray that she
has made haste, and did not delay to keep
Your commandments.

PSALM 119:59–60

———— ● ————

I pray that You, God, will teach my
daughter good judgment and knowledge,
for she believes Your commandments.

PSALM 119:66

———— ● ————

I pray, God, that Your hands have made
my daughter and fashioned her. Give her
understanding that she may learn Your
commandments.

PSALM 119:73

———— ● ————

I pray, God, that You will let Your merciful
kindness be for my daughter's comfort.

PSALM 119:76

I pray, God, that You will let my daughter's
heart be blameless regarding Your statutes,
that she may not be ashamed.

PSALM 119:80

———— ● ————

I pray, Lord God, that my daughter will
never forget Your precepts, for by them
You have given her life.

PSALM 119:93

———— ● ————

I pray that Your word, O God, is a lamp to
my daughter's feet and a light to her path.

PSALM 119:105

———— ● ————

I pray that You, God, are my daughter's
hiding place and her shield and that her
hope is in Your word.

PSALM 119:114

I pray that You, God, will give my daughter understanding that she may know Your testimonies.

PSALM 119:125

———— ● ————

I pray that my daughter's steps are directed by Your word, God, and that You let no iniquity have dominion over her.

PSALM 119:133

———— ● ————

I pray that You, Jesus, are always at my daughter's right hand, that she may not be shaken.

ACTS 2:25

———— ● ————

I pray that my daughter may gain You, Christ, and be found in You, not having her own righteousness, which is from the law, but that which is through faith in You, the righteousness which is from God by faith; that she may know You and the power of Your resurrection, and the fellowship of Your sufferings, being conformed to Your death.

PHILIPPIANS 3:8–10

———— • ————

I pray that if my daughter confesses her sins, that You, God, are faithful and just to forgive her sins and to cleanse her from all unrighteousness.

1 JOHN 1:9

———— • ————

I pray that the work of my daughter's righteousness will be peace, and the effect of her righteousness, quietness and assurance forever.

ISAIAH 32:17

———— • ————

I pray that blessed is my daughter who walks not in the counsel of the ungodly, nor stands in the path of sinners, nor sits in the seat of the scornful. But her delight

is in the law of the LORD, and in Your law
she meditates day and night. I pray that
she shall be like a tree planted by the rivers
of water, that brings forth its fruit in its
season, whose leaf also shall not wither;
and whatever she does shall prosper.

PSALM 1:1–3

———— ● ————

I pray that my daughter shall know the
truth and the truth shall make her free.

JOHN 8:32

———— ● ————

I pray that my daughter takes up Your
whole armor, God, that she may be able to
withstand in the evil day, and having done
all, to stand. I pray that she will gird her
waist with truth, that she will put on the
breastplate of righteousness, and will shod
her feet with the preparation of the gospel
of peace; and above all, take the shield of
faith with which she will be able to quench
all the fiery darts of the wicked one. I pray
that she will take the helmet of salvation,

and the sword of the Spirit, which is the
word of God; praying always with all prayer
and supplication in the Spirit, being
watchful to this end with all perseverance
and supplication for all the saints.

EPHESIANS 6:13–18

———— ● ————

I pray that my daughter will be diligent to
present herself approved to You, God, a
worker who does not need to be ashamed,
rightly dividing the word of truth.

2 TIMOTHY 2:15

———— ● ————

I pray that no one deceives my daughter
with empty words.

EPHESIANS 5:6

———— ● ————

I pray that my daughter will be a doer of
the word, and not a hearer only.

JAMES 1:22

I pray that my daughter will not be deceived, for You, God, are not mocked; for whatever she sows, that she will also reap.

GALATIANS 6:7

⬤

I pray that my daughter always remembers that all Scripture is given by inspiration of You, God, and is profitable for doctrine, for reproof, for correction, for instruction in righteousness, that the woman of God may be complete, thoroughly equipped for every good work.

2 TIMOTHY 3:16–17

21

GOD'S LOVE

Lord God, I pray that You will love my daughter in a very special way. Help her, Lord, to experience Your love through Your word and through other ways as well. Thank You, Father, in Jesus' name. Amen.

God, in accordance
with Your Word . . .

I pray that my daughter knows that love is not that she loved You, God, but that You loved her and sent Your Son to be the propitiation for her sins.

1 JOHN 4:10

———— ● ————

I pray that my daughter loves You, God, because You first loved her.

1 JOHN 4:19

I pray that You, Christ, may dwell in my
daughter's heart through faith and that
she, being rooted and grounded in love,
may be able to comprehend with all the
saints what is the width and length and
depth and height—to know Your love
which passes knowledge; that she may be
filled with all the fullness of God.

EPHESIANS 3:17–19

———— ● ————

I pray that my daughter never forgets that
You, God, demonstrated Your own love
toward her, in that while she was still a
sinner, Christ died for her.

ROMANS 5:8

———— ● ————

I pray that my daughter has Your
commandments, Jesus, and keeps them
and loves You. And because she loves You
she will be loved by God, and You will
love her and manifest Yourself to her.

JOHN 14:21

I pray that neither death nor life, nor angels nor principalities nor powers, nor things present nor things to come, nor height nor depth, nor any other created thing, shall be able to separate my daughter from the love of You, God, which is in Christ Jesus, her Lord.

ROMANS 8:38–39

I pray that You, God, so loved my daughter that You gave Your only begotten Son, that my daughter who believes in Him should not perish but have everlasting life.

JOHN 3:16

I pray that my daughter knows that You, God, have loved her with an everlasting love and with lovingkindness You have drawn her.

JEREMIAH 31:3

I pray that my daughter realizes that You, God, will rejoice over her with gladness. That You will quiet her with Your love and that You will rejoice over her with singing.

ZEPHANIAH 3:17

22
GOD'S WORD

Heavenly Father, Your word is such an important part of my life. I pray that it will be the same in my daughter's life and that Your word will be living and sharper than any two-edged sword in her life. I'm praying for Your word to be important to her. Thank You, Father, in Jesus' name, for hearing and answering my prayers for my daughter. Amen.

**God, in accordance
with Your Word . . .**

I pray, God, that in my daughter's life Your
word is living and powerful, and sharper
than any two-edged sword, piercing even
to the division of her soul and spirit, and of her
joints and marrow, and that it is a discerner
of the thoughts and intents of her heart.

HEBREWS 4:12

I pray that my daughter has been born again, not of corruptible seed but incorruptible, through Your word, God, which lives and abides forever.

1 PETER 1:23

———— ● ————

I pray that my daughter never forgets that the word of the Lord endures forever.

1 PETER 1:25

———— ● ————

I pray that my daughter puts into practice the fact that she shall not live by bread alone, but by every word that proceeds from the mouth of God.

MATTHEW 4:4

———— ● ————

I pray that my daughter will always understand and apply the fact that all Scripture is given by Your inspiration, God, and is profitable for doctrine, for reproof,

for correction, for instruction in
righteousness, that she may be complete,
thoroughly equipped for every good work.

2 TIMOTHY 3:16–17

———————— ● ————————

I pray that my daughter knows that she
has been given exceedingly great and
precious promises, that through these she
may be a partaker of the divine nature,
having escaped the corruption that is in
the world through lust.

2 PETER 1:4

———————— ● ————————

I pray that my daughter always remembers
that heaven and earth will pass away, but
Jesus' words will by no means pass away.

MATTHEW 24:35

———————— ● ————————

I pray that my daughter understands the
significance of the fact that until heaven

and earth pass away, one jot or one tittle
will by no means pass from the law till all
is fulfilled.

MATTHEW 5:18

———— ● ————

I pray that my daughter takes to heart the
fact that heaven and earth will pass away,
but Your words, Jesus, will by no means
pass away.

MARK 13:31

———— ● ————

I pray that if my daughter will abide in
Your word, Jesus, she is Your disciple
indeed. And if she does that she shall know
the truth, and the truth shall make her free.

JOHN 8:31–32

———— ● ————

I pray that my daughter's walk with You,
Lord, will be so close that her ears shall
hear a word behind her, saying, "This is the
way, walk in it."

ISAIAH 30:21

I pray that my daughter realizes the significance of the fact that You, God, said, "So shall My word be that goes forth from My mouth; it shall not return to Me void."

ISAIAH 55:11

———————— ● ————————

I pray that You, O God, will instruct my daughter and teach her in the way she should go and that You will guide her with Your eye.

PSALM 32:8

———————— ● ————————

I pray, O God, that my daughter will take Your testimonies as a heritage forever, for they are the rejoicing of her heart.

PSALM 119:111

———————— ● ————————

I pray that my daughter is Your servant, O God, and that You will give her understanding that she may know Your testimonies.

PSALM 119:125

I pray that my daughter will not be like the horse or like the mule, which have no understanding and which must be harnessed with bit and bridle, else they will not come near you.

PSALM 32:9

———— ● ————

I pray that my daughter will give attention to Your words, O God, that she will incline her ear to Your sayings. Do not let them depart from her eyes and keep them in the midst of her heart, for they are life to her when she finds them and health to her flesh.

PROVERBS 4:20–22

———— ● ————

I pray, God, that my daughter will know that every word of God is pure and that You are a shield to those who put their trust in You. I pray that she will not add to Your words, lest You rebuke her, and she be found a liar.

PROVERBS 30:5–6

I pray, God, that my daughter will not let Your Book of the Law depart from her mouth, but she shall meditate in it day and night, that she may observe to do according to all that is written in it. For then she will make her way prosperous, and then she will have good success.

JOSHUA 1:8

23

GRIEF / HURTING

God, You know the hurt in my daughter's life. And You already know other hurts that are yet to come to her. By and through Your word I pray that You will console my daughter in a very special way. Wipe away her tears and bring joy back into her life. I pray Your own words for those results. Please hear and honor them in Jesus' name. Amen.

God, in accordance with Your Word . . .

I pray that You, God, will console my daughter who mourns and give her beauty for ashes, the oil of joy for mourning, the garment of praise for the spirit of heaviness so that she may be called a tree of righteousness.

ISAIAH 61:3

I pray, O God, that You will comfort my
daughter in all her tribulations, that she
may be able to comfort those who are in
any trouble, with the comfort with which
she herself is comforted by You.

2 CORINTHIANS 1:4

I pray that my daughter is blessed when
she mourns for she shall be comforted.

MATTHEW 5:4

I pray that my daughter will not be ignorant
concerning those who have fallen asleep,
lest she sorrow as others who have
no hope.

1 THESSALONIANS 4:13

I pray, O God, that You have comforted
my daughter and will have mercy on her
affliction.

ISAIAH 49:13

I pray that when my daughter passes through the waters, You, God, will be with her and through the rivers, they shall not overflow her. When she walks through the fire, she shall not be burned, nor shall the flame scorch her.

ISAIAH 43:2

———— ● ————

I pray that the Lord Jesus Christ Himself, and her God and Father, who has loved my daughter and given her everlasting consolation and good hope by grace, will comfort her heart and establish her in every good word and work.

2 THESSALONIANS 2:16–17

———— ● ————

I pray that though my daughter may walk through the valley of the shadow of death, she will fear no evil; for You, God, are with her and Your rod and Your staff, they comfort her.

PSALM 23:4

I pray that my daughter always remembers
that in You, Jesus, she does not have a
High Priest who cannot sympathize with
her weaknesses, but was in all points
tempted as she is, yet without sin. Let her
therefore come boldly to the throne of
grace, that she may obtain mercy and find
grace to help in time of need.

HEBREWS 4:15–16

●

I pray that You, God, will wipe away every
tear from my daughter's eyes and that there
shall be no more death, nor sorrow, nor
crying. I pray that there shall be no more
pain, for the former things have passed
away.

REVELATION 21:4

●

I pray that in this crucial time in my
daughter's life she can say, "O Death, where
is your sting? O Hades, where is your
victory?"

1 CORINTHIANS 15:55

I pray that this is my daughter's comfort in her affliction, that Your word, God, has given her life.

PSALM 119:50

———— ● ————

I pray that my daughter will cast all her cares upon You, O God, for You care for her.

1 PETER 5:7

———— ● ————

I pray that my daughter will fear not, for You, God, are with her. I pray that she will be not dismayed, for You are her God. I pray that You will strengthen her and help her and that You will uphold her with Your righteous right hand.

ISAIAH 41:10

———— ● ————

I pray that my daughter shall obtain joy and gladness and that sorrow and sighing shall flee away.

ISAIAH 51:11

I pray that my daughter will walk by faith
and not by sight and that she is confident,
yes, well pleased rather to be absent from
the body and to be present with You, Lord.

2 CORINTHIANS 5:8

24

INHERITANCE

Lord God, in Your Son's name and through Your perfect word I pray that my daughter will be fully aware of and never forget the magnitude of the inheritance that awaits her. Give her a vision of that inheritance as even now I pray Your words for her. Thank You, God, in Jesus' name. Amen.

God, in accordance with Your Word . . .

I pray that whatever my daughter does, she will do it heartily, as to You, Lord, and not to men, knowing that from You she will receive the reward of the inheritance; for she serves the Lord Christ.

COLOSSIANS 3:23–24

———————— ● ————————

I pray that my daughter has been given exceedingly great and precious promises, that through these she may be a partaker of the divine nature, having escaped the corruption that is in the world through lust.

2 PETER 1:4

———— ● ————

I pray that my daughter has an inheritance incorruptible and undefiled and that does not fade away, reserved in heaven for her.

1 PETER 1:4

———— ● ————

I commend my daughter to You, God, and to the word of Your grace, which is able to build her up and give her an inheritance among all those who are sanctified.

ACTS 20:32

———— ● ————

I pray, God, that the Spirit Himself bears witness with my spirit that my daughter is a child of Yours and if a child, then an heir—an heir of Yours and a joint heir with

Christ, if indeed she suffers with Him, that she may also be glorified together with Him.

ROMANS 8:16–17

————————— ● —————————

I pray that my daughter in You, Jesus, has obtained an inheritance, being predestined according to the purpose of Him who works all things according to the counsel of His will, that she who first trusted in You should be to the praise of His glory. In You, Jesus, she also trusted, after she heard the word of truth, the gospel of your salvation; in whom also, having believed, she was sealed with the Holy Spirit of promise, who is the guarantee of our inheritance until the redemption of the purchased possession, to the praise of His glory.

EPHESIANS 1:11–14

————————— ● —————————

I pray that my daughter always remembers that in Your house, God, are many mansions and if it were not so, Jesus

would have told her. Help her to remember
that Jesus has gone to prepare a place for
her and if He goes and prepares a place
for her He will come again and receive her
to Himself, that where He is, there she may
be also.

JOHN 14:2–3

———————— ● ————————

I pray, Lord, that my daughter is aware that
eye has not seen, nor ear heard, nor have
entered into her heart the things which
You have prepared for those who love You.

1 CORINTHIANS 2:9

3.3.16 Lord I am so thankful
for Your word & it's power!
I am blessed by these promises!

25

LONELY

Jesus, I pray to You concerning any feeling of being lonely that my daughter may be experiencing now or may experience in the future. As I pray Your words, help her to remember that You said You would be with her always and that You are her constant companion. I pray Your very words to this end. In Your name I pray. Amen.

God, in accordance with Your Word . . .

I pray that my daughter's conduct will be without covetousness, and that she will be content with such things as she has. For You, God, said, "I will never leave you nor forsake you."

HEBREWS 13:5

———————— ● ————————

I pray that my daughter will fear not, for You, God, are with her. That she be not dismayed, for You are her God. I pray that

You will strengthen her and that You will
help her and that You will uphold her with
Your righteous right hand.

ISAIAH 41:10

———— ● ————

I pray that my daughter realizes that You,
God, count the number of the stars and
call them all by name. I pray that she
remembers that great is her Lord and
mighty in power and that Your
understanding is infinite.

PSALM 147:4–5

———— ● ————

I pray, God, that neither death nor life, nor
angels nor principalities nor powers, nor
things present nor things to come, nor
height nor depth, nor any other created
thing, shall be able to separate my daughter
from Your love, God, which is in Christ
Jesus her Lord.

ROMANS 8:38–39

I pray that my daughter remembers Jesus'
promise to be with her always, even to the
end of the age.

MATTHEW 28:20

●

I pray, Jesus, that my daughter remembers
Your promise that You will not leave her as
an orphan but that You will come to her.

JOHN 14:18

●

I pray that my daughter will be strong and
of good courage and that she does not
fear nor is she afraid, for You, the LORD
her God, You are the One who goes with
her. I pray that You will not leave her nor
forsake her.

DEUTERONOMY 31:6

●

I pray that if even I forsake my daughter,
then You, LORD, will take care of her.

PSALM 27:10

I pray that though the mountains shall
depart and the hills be removed, Your
kindness, God, shall not depart from my
daughter, nor shall Your covenant of peace
be removed from her.

ISAIAH 54:10

●

I pray, O God, that You are my daughter's
refuge and strength and a very present
help in trouble.

PSALM 46:1

26

LOVE

God, Your word tells us that You are love and that we must love others even as You have loved us. This is such an important matter that I want to pray to You on my daughter's behalf. Honor Your words, Lord, as my prayers for my daughter. Thank You for the privilege of praying in Jesus' name. Amen.

God, in accordance
with Your Word . . .

I pray that my daughter will love others, for love is of You, God.

1 JOHN 4:7

———— ● ————

I pray that my daughter understands the true meaning of love and that though she speaks with the tongues of men and of angels, but has not love, she has become sounding brass or a clanging cymbal. And though she has the gift of prophecy, and understands all mysteries and all knowledge, and though she has all faith, so that she can remove mountains, but has not love, she is nothing. And though she bestows all her goods to feed the poor, and though she gives her body to be burned, but has not love, it profits her nothing. I pray that she remembers that love suffers long and is kind; love does not envy; love does not parade itself, is not puffed up; does not behave rudely, does not seek its own, is not provoked, thinks no evil; does not rejoice in iniquity, but rejoices in the truth; bears all things, believes all things, hopes all things, endures all things. Help her to understand that love never fails. Help her to abide in faith, hope, love, these three; but the greatest of these is love.

1 CORINTHIANS 13:1–8, 13

———— ● ————

I pray that my daughter understands that love is not that she loved You, God, but that You loved her and sent Your Son to be

the propitiation for her sins. And help her
to know that if You so loved her, she also
ought to love others.

1 JOHN 4:10–11

———————— ● ————————

I pray that my daughter totally understands
that as You, God, loved Jesus, He also has
loved her and she is to abide in His love.

JOHN 15:9

———————— ● ————————

I pray that if my daughter has Jesus'
commandments and keeps them, it is she
who loves Him. And my daughter who
loves Jesus will be loved by You, God, and
Jesus will love her and manifest Himself to
her.

JOHN 14:21

———————— ● ————————

I pray, God, that You have loved my
daughter with an everlasting love and with
lovingkindness have drawn her to You.

JEREMIAH 31:3

I pray that You, God, will bring to my daughter's mind that it is Jesus' commandment that she love others just as He has loved her.

JOHN 15:12

●

I pray that my daughter shall love You, the Lord her God, with all her heart, with all her soul, with all her mind, and with all her strength and that she shall love her neighbor as herself.

MARK 12:30–31

●

I pray that neither death nor life, nor angels nor principalities nor powers, nor things present nor things to come, nor height nor depth, nor any other created thing, shall be able to separate my daughter from Your love, God, which is in Christ Jesus her Lord.

ROMANS 8:38–39

I pray that You, God, love my daughter, because she has loved Jesus, and has believed that He came forth from You.

JOHN 16:27

●

I pray that my daughter will realize that You, God, demonstrated Your own love toward her in that while she was still a sinner, Christ died for her.

ROMANS 5:8

●

I pray that You, God, so loved my daughter that You gave Your only begotten Son, that she who believes in Him should not perish but have everlasting life.

JOHN 3:16

●

I pray that my daughter has known and believed the love that You, God, have for her and that she who loves You must love her brother also.

1 JOHN 4:16, 21

I pray, Jesus, that my daughter will take heed to the new commandment You gave to her that she love others as You have loved her and that by this all will know that she is Your disciple, if she has love for others.

JOHN 13:34–35

27

LOVE FOR MY DAUGHTER

Lord, I pray these Your words for my daughter.
Honor my prayers by honoring Your own words. I
praise You and pray to You in Jesus' name. Amen.

**God, in accordance
with Your Word . . .**

I pray that while my daughter and I have
not seen You, God, at any time, if we love
one another, You abide in us, and Your
love has been perfected in us.

1 JOHN 4:12

———————— ● ————————

I pray, Lord Jesus, that by this my daughter
and I know love, because You laid down
Your life for us. And we also ought to lay
down our lives for each other.

1 JOHN 3:16

I pray, Jesus, that my daughter and I will
follow Your commandment that we love
one another as You have loved us.

JOHN 15:12

———— • ————

I pray that if You, God, so loved my
daughter and me, we also ought to love
one another.

1 JOHN 4:11

———— • ————

I pray, Lord God, that my daughter and I
will love one another, for love is of
You; and everyone who loves is born of
You and knows You. But if we do not love
we do not know You, for You are love.

1 JOHN 4:7–8

———— • ————

I pray, Jesus, that my daughter and I will
follow Your command that we love one
another.

JOHN 15:17

I pray, Lord Jesus, that my daughter and I always remember that when we were still without strength, in due time You died for us.

ROMANS 5:6

———————— ● ————————

I pray that my daughter and I will always understand the significance of the question, "Can two walk together, unless they are agreed?"

AMOS 3:3

28

NEEDS

Lord, You and You alone know all of my daughter's needs. I desire now to spend time with You praying Your word over her needs and to ask You to bless the praying of Your word and to honor the praying of Your word by meeting my daughter's needs as only You can do. I pray Your words now in Jesus' name. Amen.

God, in accordance with Your Word . . .

I pray that my daughter will delight herself also in You, LORD, and that You will give her the desires of her heart.

PSALM 37:4

---•---

I pray that You, God, will open Your hand and satisfy the desire of my daughter.

PSALM 145:16

I pray that You, LORD, will guide my
daughter continually.

ISAIAH 58:11

———— ● ————

I pray that my daughter will not spend
wages for what does not satisfy and that
she will listen carefully to You, God, and
will let her soul delight itself in abundance.

ISAIAH 55:2

———— ● ————

I pray that whatever things my daughter
asks in prayer, believing, she will receive.

MATTHEW 21:22

———— ● ————

I pray, Lord Jesus, that if my daughter
abides in You and Your words abide in her,
she will ask what she desires, and it shall
be done for her.

JOHN 15:7

I pray, Jesus, that if my daughter asks anything in Your name, You will do it.

JOHN 14:14

———— • ————

I pray that my daughter will ask in Your name, Jesus, and she will receive, that her joy may be full.

JOHN 16:24

———— • ————

I pray that my daughter shall know the truth and the truth shall make her free.

JOHN 8:32

———— • ————

I pray that if my daughter's heart does not condemn her, she has confidence toward You, God. And whatever she asks she receives from You, because she keeps Your commandments and does those things that are pleasing in Your sight.

1 JOHN 3:21–22

I pray that You, the God and Father of our Lord Jesus Christ, bless my daughter with every spiritual blessing in the heavenly places in Christ.

EPHESIANS 1:3

———————— ● ————————

I pray that my daughter can do all things through Christ who strengthens her.

PHILIPPIANS 4:13

———————— ● ————————

I pray that You, my God, shall supply all my daughter's needs according to Your riches in glory by Christ Jesus.

PHILIPPIANS 4:19

29

OBEDIENCE

God, You have said that obedience is more important to You than is sacrifice. Because I believe that
You meant what You said, I ask You to help my
daughter be obedient to You in every way and in
every situation. Having asked You for it in Jesus'
name, I believe that it will happen, and I thank You
in His name. Amen.

**God, in accordance
with Your Word . . .**

I pray that my daughter recognizes the fact
that You, God, have set before her today a
blessing and a curse: the blessing, if she
obeys the commandments of her Lord, her
God, which You have commanded her
today; and the curse, if she does not obey
the commandments of the Lord her God,
but turns aside from the way which You
command her today, to go after other gods
which she has not known.

DEUTERONOMY 11:26–28

I pray that my daughter never forgets that to obey is better than sacrifice.

1 SAMUEL 15:22

———— • ————

I pray that my daughter will heed Your commandments, O God, so that her peace will be like a river and her righteousness like the waves of the sea.

ISAIAH 48:18

———— • ————

I pray, O God, that my daughter will obey Your voice, and You will be her God, and she shall be Your child. And that she will walk in all the ways that You have commanded her, that it may be well with her.

JEREMIAH 7:23

———— • ————

I pray, Lord Jesus, that my daughter loves You and keeps Your commandments.

JOHN 14:15

I pray, God, that my daughter knows that
she ought to obey You rather than people.

ACTS 5:29

———— ● ————

I pray, Jesus, that my daughter will always
keep Your commandments.

1 JOHN 2:3

———— ● ————

I pray that my daughter will walk in Your
ways, God, to keep Your statutes and Your
commandments, and that You will lengthen
her days.

1 KINGS 3:14

———— ● ————

I pray that my daughter will learn Your
statutes, O God, and be careful to observe
them. I pray that she will be careful to do
as You, the LORD her God, have commanded
her and that she shall not turn aside to the
right hand or to the left. I pray that she will
walk in all the ways which You have

commanded her, that she may live and
that it may be well with her, and that You
may prolong her days.

DEUTERONOMY 5:1, 32–33

———— ● ————

I pray that whatever my daughter does,
she does it heartily, as to the Lord and not
to men.

COLOSSIANS 3:23

———— ● ————

I pray that You, God, will teach my
daughter to do Your will, for You are her
God.

PSALM 143:10

30
PATIENCE

Lord Jesus, patience is so important but so elusive.
I pray to You now what You have already declared
in Your word and I ask You to honor it in my
daughter's life. Bless now the praying of Your word.
Amen.

God, in accordance
with Your Word . . .

I pray that whatever things were written
for my daughter's learning, that she
through the patience and comfort of the
Scriptures might have hope. Now may You,
the God of patience and comfort, grant
my daughter to be like-minded toward
others, according to Christ Jesus.

ROMANS 15:4–5

———————— • ————————

I pray that my daughter will glory in
tribulations, knowing that tribulation

produces perseverance; and perseverance,
character; and character, hope.

ROMANS 5:3–4

———— ● ————

I pray that my daughter will wait patiently
for You, Lord, and that You will incline
Yourself to her and hear her cry.

PSALM 40:1

———— ● ————

I pray that my daughter will imitate those
who through faith and patience inherit the
promises.

HEBREWS 6:12

———— ● ————

I pray that my daughter will rest in You,
Lord, and that she will wait patiently for
You. I pray that she does not fret because
of someone who prospers or because of
someone who brings wicked schemes to
pass. I pray that she will cease from anger,

and forsake wrath and that she does not
fret—it only causes harm.

PSALM 37:7–8

———— ● ————

I pray that my daughter does not cast away
her confidence, which has great reward.
For she has need of endurance, so that
after she has done Your will, God, she may
receive her promise.

HEBREWS 10:35–36

———— ● ————

I pray that since my daughter is surrounded
by so great a cloud of witnesses, she will lay
aside every weight, and the sin which so
easily ensnares her, and will run with
endurance the race that is set before her.

HEBREWS 12:1

———— ● ————

I pray that my daughter will not hasten in
her spirit to be angry, for anger rests in the
bosom of fools.

ECCLESIASTES 7:9

I pray that the fruit of the Spirit in my daughter is love, joy, peace, longsuffering, kindness, goodness, faithfulness, gentleness, and self-control.

GALATIANS 5:22–23

I pray that my daughter will wait on You, LORD, and that she shall renew her strength. I pray that she shall mount up with wings like eagles, she shall run and not be weary, and that she shall walk and not faint.

ISAIAH 40:31

I pray that my daughter will wait on You, LORD, and that she will be of good courage. I also pray that You will strengthen her heart and that she will wait on You.

PSALM 27:14

I pray that my daughter will hope and wait quietly for Your salvation, O LORD.

LAMENTATIONS 3:26

I pray that my daughter will hope for what she does not see and eagerly wait for it with perseverance.

ROMANS 8:25

I pray that my daughter understands that the testing of her faith produces patience and that she should let patience have its perfect work, that she may be perfect and complete, lacking nothing.

JAMES 1:3–4

I pray that my daughter will be patient until Your coming, Lord. I pray that she will see how the farmer waits for the precious fruit of the earth, waiting patiently for it until it receives the early and latter rain and that she also will be patient, for Your coming is near.

JAMES 5:7–8

31

PEACE

Heavenly Father, just as Your word says, I pray perfect peace for my daughter. There is no process that I know of that is more important to her having peace than to pray Your words of promised peace to her. It is Your words that I pray in Jesus' name and I thank You for hearing and answering these my prayers. Amen.

God, in accordance
with Your Word . . .

I pray, God, that You will keep my daughter
in perfect peace, whose mind is stayed on
You, because she trusts in You.

ISAIAH 26:3

I pray that Jesus Himself is my daughter's
peace.

EPHESIANS 2:14

I pray that my daughter will lie down in peace, and sleep; for You alone, O LORD, make her dwell in safety.

PSALM 4:8

———— ● ————

I pray, O LORD, that You will give strength to my daughter and that You will bless her with peace.

PSALM 29:11

———— ● ————

I pray that You, Jesus, have left Your peace with my daughter. I pray that her heart will not be troubled, neither will she be afraid.

JOHN 14:27

———— ● ————

I pray that Your kindness, God, shall not depart from my daughter, nor shall Your covenant of peace be removed from her.

ISAIAH 54:10

I pray that my daughter who has been justified by faith, will have peace with You, God, through her Lord Jesus Christ.

ROMANS 5:1

———— • ————

I pray that my daughter will be anxious for nothing, but in everything by prayer and supplication, with thanksgiving, will let her requests be made known to You, God; and Your peace which surpasses all understanding, will guard her heart and mind through Christ Jesus.

PHILIPPIANS 4:6–7

———— • ————

I pray, God, that the peace of God will rule in my daughter's heart.

COLOSSIANS 3:15

32

POWER

Lord God, my daughter is in need of Your power. That power comes only through Your word and that is what I pray to You today. Honor the praying of Your word and bring Your power into the life of my daughter. It is in the powerful name of Jesus that I offer up Your words to You in prayer for my daughter. Thank You for hearing and answering each of these prayers. Amen.

God, in accordance with Your Word . . .

I pray that my daughter will take pleasure in infirmities, in reproaches, in needs, in persecutions, in distresses, for Christ's sake. For when she is weak, then she is strong.

2 CORINTHIANS 12:10

———— • ————

I pray that my daughter can do all things through Christ who strengthens her.

PHILIPPIANS 4:13

I pray that in all things my daughter is more than a conqueror through Jesus who loved her.

ROMANS 8:37

●

I pray, Jesus, that whatever my daughter asks in Your name that You will do, that the Father may be glorified in the Son.

JOHN 14:13

●

I pray that You, God, are able to make all grace abound toward my daughter, that she, always having all sufficiency in all things, may have an abundance for every good work.

2 CORINTHIANS 9:8

●

I pray, Jesus, that Your grace is sufficient for my daughter, for Your strength is made perfect in weakness.

2 CORINTHIANS 12:9

I pray that my daughter will see the exceeding greatness of Your power, God, toward the one who believes, according to the working of Your mighty power.

EPHESIANS 1:19

———— ● ————

I pray, O God, that You are able to do exceedingly abundantly above all that my daughter asks or thinks, according to the power that works in her.

EPHESIANS 3:20

33

PRAISE

Heavenly Father, we were created to praise You. Through the praying of Your word I petition You to put into my daughter's heart a consistent desire to praise You at all times. These words of Yours are my prayers in Jesus' name. Amen.

God, in accordance with Your Word . . .

I pray, Lord God, that my daughter will sing praises to You and that she will declare Your deeds among the people.

PSALM 9:11

———— ● ————

I pray that my daughter will sing praises to You, LORD, as long as she lives.

PSALM 104:33

I pray that every day my daughter will bless
You, God, and will praise Your name
forever and ever.

PSALM 145:2

●

I pray that my daughter will know that
great is the LORD, and greatly to be praised
and that Your greatness is unsearchable.

PSALM 145:3

●

I pray that my daughter's tongue shall speak
of Your righteousness, Lord, and of Your
praise all the day long.

PSALM 35:28

●

I pray, O LORD, that You will open my
daughter's lips and her mouth shall show
forth Your praise.

PSALM 51:15

I pray, O LORD, that my daughter will praise
You.

ISAIAH 12:1

———— ● ————

I pray that my daughter will give You
thanks, O Lord God Almighty, the One
who is and who was and who is to come,
because You have taken Your great power
and reigned.

REVELATION 11:17

———— ● ————

I pray that my daughter will hope
continually, O God, and will praise You yet
more and more.

PSALM 71:14

———— ● ————

I pray, God, that my daughter will enter
into Your gates with thanksgiving and into
Your courts with praise.

PSALM 100:4

I pray that You, LORD, are my daughter's
strength and song and that You have
become her salvation; that You are her
God, and that she will praise You.

EXODUS 15:2

———— ● ————

I pray that my daughter will proclaim the
name of the LORD and ascribe greatness to
You her God.

DEUTERONOMY 32:3

———— ● ————

I pray that my daughter will proclaim, "The
LORD lives! Blessed be my Rock! Let God
be exalted, the Rock of my salvation!"

2 SAMUEL 22:47

———— ● ————

I pray that my daughter always remembers
that You, LORD, are great and greatly to be
praised.

1 CHRONICLES 16:25

I pray that my daughter will bless You, LORD,
at all times and that Your praise shall
continually be in her mouth.

PSALM 34:1

———— ● ————

I pray, God, that You have put a new song
in my daughter's mouth—praise to her
God.

PSALM 40:3

———— ● ————

I pray that my daughter realizes that great
is the LORD and greatly to be praised.

PSALM 48:1

———— ● ————

I pray that my daughter prays, "Blessed be
the Lord, who daily loads me with benefits."

PSALM 68:19

———— ● ————

I pray that You will let my daughter's soul
live, O God, and it shall praise You.

PSALM 119:175

I pray that my daughter will give thanks to You, LORD, for You are good! For Your mercy endures forever.

PSALM 106:1

———— • ————

I pray that my daughter will praise You, God, for she is fearfully and wonderfully made. Marvelous are Your works, and that her soul knows very well.

PSALM 139:14

———— • ————

I pray that my daughter's mouth shall speak the praise of You, God.

PSALM 145:21

———— • ————

I pray that my daughter will praise You, God, for Your mighty acts and that she will praise You according to Your excellent greatness.

PSALM 150:2

I pray that my daughter will praise You,
Lord!

PSALM 146:1

I pray that my daughter will continually
offer the sacrifice of praise to You, God,
that is, the fruit of her lips, giving thanks to
Your name.

HEBREWS 13:15

34

PROTECTION

Lord God, honor the prayers I lift up to You for my daughter's protection. Protect her at all times through the praying of Your word in Jesus' name. Amen.

**God, in accordance
with Your Word . . .**

I pray that my daughter's LORD God, who goes before her, will fight for her.

DEUTERONOMY 1:30

———————— ● ————————

I pray that Jesus has given my daughter the authority to trample on serpents and scorpions, and over all the power of the enemy, and nothing shall by any means hurt her.

LUKE 10:19

I pray that no weapon formed against my daughter shall prosper and every tongue which rises against her in judgment, You, God, shall condemn.

ISAIAH 54:17

———— • ————

I pray that if my daughter will indeed obey Your voice, God, and do all that You speak, then You will be an enemy to her enemies and an adversary to her adversaries.

EXODUS 23:22

———— • ————

I pray that You, Lord, are faithful, who will establish my daughter and guard her from the evil one.

2 THESSALONIANS 3:3

———— • ————

I pray that if God is for my daughter, who can be against her?

ROMANS 8:31

35

REBELLIOUS

Lord God, through the power of Your word I pray that You will keep my daughter free from any rebellious spirit or attitude. I thank You in Jesus' precious name. Amen.

God, in accordance with Your Word . . .

I pray that my daughter, by doing good, may put to silence the ignorance of foolish men.

1 PETER 2:15

———————— ● ————————

I pray that my daughter will gird up the loins of her mind, be sober, and rest her hope fully upon the grace that is to be brought to her at the revelation of Jesus Christ; as an obedient child, not conforming herself to the former lusts, as

in her ignorance; but as You, God, who
called her is holy, she also is to be holy in
all her conduct.

1 PETER 1:13–15

———— ● ————

I pray that my daughter is aware that
rebellion is as the sin of witchcraft.

1 SAMUEL 15:23

———— ● ————

I pray that my daughter will obey those
who rule over her, and be submissive, for
they watch out for her soul, as those who
must give account.

HEBREWS 13:17

———— ● ————

I pray that my daughter will be like Jesus
and humble herself and become obedient.

PHILIPPIANS 2:8

I pray that if my daughter is willing and obedient she shall eat the good of the land.

ISAIAH 1:19

———— ● ————

I pray that like You, Jesus, my daughter learns obedience by the things which she suffers.

HEBREWS 5:8

———— ● ————

I pray, God, that my daughter knows that You resist the proud but give grace to the humble and that she will humble herself under Your mighty hand, that You, God, may exalt her in due time.

1 PETER 5:5–6

———— ● ————

I pray that my daughter knows and understands that no grave trouble will overtake the righteous, but the wicked shall be filled with evil.

PROVERBS 12:21

I pray that my daughter will submit to You,
God. That she will resist the devil and he
will flee from her.

JAMES 4:7

———————— ● ————————

I pray that while my daughter was once
darkness, now she is light in the Lord and
that she will walk as a child of the light.

EPHESIANS 5:8

———————— ● ————————

I pray that my daughter will no longer walk
in the futility of her mind.

EPHESIANS 4:17

———————— ● ————————

I pray that my daughter does not let sin
reign in her mortal body, that she should
obey it in its lusts. I also pray that she does
not present herself to sin, but that she
presents herself to You, God, as being alive

from the dead, and her members as instruments of righteousness to God. For sin shall not have dominion over her, for she is not under law but under grace.

ROMANS 6:12–14

36

SALVATION

Lord, the most important thing in life is salvation. I pray for my daughter's salvation through the powerful praying of Your Holy Word. Hear these my prayers for my daughter. Honor them. And bless her with Your salvation. In Jesus' name I pray. Amen.

**God, in accordance
with Your Word . . .**

I pray that my daughter will discover that Jesus said, "He who believes in Me has everlasting life."

JOHN 6:47

———— • ————

I pray that my daughter remembers that Jesus has come to seek and to save that which was lost.

LUKE 19:10

I pray, Lord Jesus, that my daughter will
come to understand what You meant when
You said, "Therefore whoever confesses
Me before men, him I will also confess
before My Father who is in heaven."

MATTHEW 10:32

———————— ● ————————

I pray that if my daughter will confess with
her mouth the Lord Jesus and believe in
her heart that God raised Him from the
dead, she will be saved. For with her heart
she believes to righteousness, and with her
mouth confession is made to salvation.

ROMANS 10:9–10

———————— ● ————————

I pray that You, God, have saved my
daughter and called her with a holy
calling, not according to her works, but
according to Your own purpose and grace
which was given to her in Christ Jesus
before time began.

2 TIMOTHY 1:9

I pray that You, God, so loved my daughter
that You gave Your only begotten Son, that
if my daughter believes in Him she should
not perish but have everlasting life.

JOHN 3:16

———— ● ————

I pray that You did not send Your Son into
the world to condemn my daughter, but
that my daughter through Him might be
saved.

JOHN 3:17

———— ● ————

I pray that this will be my daughter's
testimony: that You, God, have given her
eternal life, and this life is in Your Son.

1 JOHN 5:11

———— ● ————

I pray that by grace my daughter has been
saved through faith, and that not of herself;
it is the gift of God, not of works, lest she
should boast.

EPHESIANS 2:8–9

I pray, God, that it is not by works of righteousness which my daughter has done, but according to Your mercy You saved her, through the washing of regeneration and renewing of the Holy Spirit whom You poured out on her abundantly through Jesus Christ her Savior.

TITUS 3:5–6

———— ● ————

I pray, God, that Jesus stands at the door and knocks and if my daughter hears His voice and opens the door, He will come in to her and dine with her, and her with Him.

REVELATION 3:20

———— ● ————

I pray, God, that my daughter has been born again, not of corruptible seed but incorruptible, through Your word which lives and abides forever.

1 PETER 1:23

37

SATAN DEFEATED

Heavenly Father, my daughter's enemy is Satan. He wants to destroy her. But God, Your word is stronger than even Satan and that is what I pray on my daughter's behalf. I pray Your word that she will defeat every attack of Satan in her life. God, please honor the praying of Your word to the defeat of Satan in her life. Thank You, God, in the powerful name of Jesus. Amen.

God, in accordance
with Your Word . . .

I pray that my daughter will be strong in You, Lord, and the power of Your might. I pray that she will put on the whole armor of God, that she may be able to stand against the wiles of the devil. For she does not wrestle against flesh and blood, but against principalities, against powers, against the rulers of the darkness of this age, against spiritual hosts of wickedness in the heavenly places. I pray that she will take up Your whole armor, God, that she may be able to withstand in the evil day, and having done all, to stand. I pray that she has girded her waist with truth, having put on the breastplate of righteousness, and having shod her feet with the preparation of the gospel of peace and above all, taking the shield of faith with which she will be able to quench all the fiery darts of the wicked one. I pray that she also takes the helmet of salvation, and the sword of the Spirit, which is the word of God; praying always with all prayer and supplication in the Spirit, being watchful to this end with all perseverance and supplication for all the saints.

EPHESIANS 6:10–18

———— ● ————

I pray, God, that my daughter understands that even the angels who did not keep their proper domain, but left their own abode, You have reserved in everlasting chains under darkness for the judgment of the great day.

JUDE 1:6

I pray that You, God, will open my
daughter's eyes, in order to turn them
from darkness to light, and from the
power of Satan to You, that she may
receive forgiveness of sins and an
inheritance among those who are
sanctified by faith in Jesus.

ACTS 26:18

———— ● ————

I pray, God, that You preserve the soul of
my daughter and deliver her out of the
hand of the wicked.

PSALM 97:10

———— ● ————

I pray, God, for my daughter that the Son
of God was manifested that He might
destroy the works of the devil.

1 JOHN 3:8

———— ● ————

I pray for my daughter that she puts off,
concerning her former conduct, the old

woman which grows corrupt according to the deceitful lusts, and be renewed in the spirit of her mind and that she put on the new woman which was created according to You, God, in true righteousness and holiness.

EPHESIANS 4:22–24

————————— ● —————————

I pray that my daughter is strong, and that the word of God abides in her and she has overcome the wicked one.

1 JOHN 2:14

————————— ● —————————

I pray that my daughter will not give place to the devil.

EPHESIANS 4:27

————————— ● —————————

I do not pray, God, that You should take my daughter out of the world, but that You should keep her from the evil one.

JOHN 17:15

I pray, Jesus, that my daughter knows that
You have disarmed principalities and
powers, and have made a public spectacle
of them, triumphing over them in it.

COLOSSIANS 2:15

———————————— ● ————————————

I pray that my daughter will be sober
and vigilant, because her adversary the
devil walks about like a roaring lion,
seeking whom he may devour. I pray that
she will resist him, steadfast in the faith,
knowing that the same sufferings are
experienced by other Christians in the
world.

1 PETER 5:8–9

———————————— ● ————————————

I pray that at this time my daughter will
remember that Jesus went about doing
good and healing all who were oppressed
by the devil, for God was with Him.

ACTS 10:38

I pray that my daughter will submit to You,
God, and that she will resist the devil and
he will flee from her.

JAMES 4:7

———————— ● ————————

I pray that You, God, have delivered my
daughter from the power of darkness and
conveyed her into the kingdom of Jesus,
in whom she has redemption through His
blood, the forgiveness of sins.

COLOSSIANS 1:13–14

———————— ● ————————

I pray that in all things my daughter is more
than a conqueror through Him who loved
her.

ROMANS 8:37

———————— ● ————————

I pray, God, that the accuser of my daughter,
who accuses her before her God day and
night, has been cast down. I pray that she

overcame him by the blood of the Lamb
and by the word of her testimony.

REVELATION 12:10–11

———— ● ————

I pray that neither death nor life, nor angels
nor principalities nor powers, nor things
present nor things to come, nor height nor
depth, nor any other created thing, shall
be able to separate my daughter from the
love of God which is in Christ Jesus her
Lord.

ROMANS 8:38–39

———— ● ————

I pray that while my daughter is hard
pressed on every side, yet she is not
crushed; she is perplexed, but not in
despair; persecuted, but not forsaken;
struck down, but not destroyed—always
carrying about in her body the dying of
the Lord Jesus, that the life of Jesus
also may be manifested in her body.

2 CORINTHIANS 4:8–10

I pray that though my daughter walks in
the flesh, she does not war according to
the flesh. For the weapons of her warfare
are not carnal but mighty in God for
pulling down strongholds, casting down
arguments and every high thing that exalts
itself against the knowledge of God,
bringing every thought into captivity to
the obedience of Christ.

2 CORINTHIANS 10:3–5

●

I pray that my daughter has her senses
exercised to discern both good and evil.

HEBREWS 5:14

●

I pray, Lord, that You will guard my daughter
from the evil one.

2 THESSALONIANS 3:3

●

I pray, God, that Your Presence will go with
my daughter forever.

EXODUS 33:14

I pray, God, that my daughter will be strong and of good courage; that she will not be afraid, nor dismayed, for You, the Lord her God, are with her wherever she goes.

JOSHUA 1:9

———— ● ————

I pray, God, that You will preserve the soul of my daughter and that You will deliver her out of the hand of the wicked.

PSALM 97:10

———— ● ————

I pray, God, that You are my daughter's refuge and that You will thrust out the enemy from before her.

DEUTERONOMY 33:27

———— ● ————

I pray, God, that the angel of the Lord encamps all around my daughter who fears You, and delivers her.

PSALM 34:7

I pray that Satan will not take advantage of my daughter for she is not ignorant of his devices.

2 CORINTHIANS 2:11

———— ● ————

I pray that my daughter knows that she does not live by bread alone but by every word that proceeds from the mouth of God.

MATTHEW 4:4

———— ● ————

I pray, Lord, that my daughter will drive Satan away by worshiping the Lord her God, and Him only she shall serve.

MATTHEW 4:10

———— ● ————

I pray that my daughter will gird up the loins of her mind and be sober, and rest her hope fully upon the grace that is to be brought to her at the revelation of Jesus Christ, as an obedient child, not

conforming herself to the former lusts, as
in her ignorance; but as You, God, who
called her are holy, may she also be holy in
all her conduct.

1 PETER 1:13–15

●

I pray that my daughter will have the mind
of Christ.

1 CORINTHIANS 2:16

38

SECURITY

Lord, real and true security comes only from You. I pray Your words concerning security for my daughter. Through the praying of Your word help her to sense the security that only You can give. Lord, I thank You and I pray in Your name. Amen.

God, in accordance
with Your Word . . .

I pray that surely goodness and mercy shall follow my daughter all the days of her life and that she will dwell in the house of the LORD forever.

PSALM 23:6

———— ● ————

I pray that my daughter is one of those who has come to You, Jesus, and who You will by no means cast out.

JOHN 6:37

I pray that my daughter is persuaded that neither death nor life, nor angels nor principalities nor powers, nor things present nor things to come, nor height nor depth, nor any other created thing, shall be able to separate her from the love of God which is in Christ Jesus her Lord.

ROMANS 8:38–39

I pray that in Jesus my daughter also trusted, after she heard the word of truth, the gospel of her salvation, in whom also, having believed, she was sealed with the Holy Spirit of promise.

EPHESIANS 1:13

I pray, Jesus, that my daughter has heard Your voice and that You know her, and that she follows You and that You will give her eternal life, and she shall never perish.

JOHN 10:27–28

I pray that my daughter does not grieve
the Holy Spirit of God, by whom she was
sealed for the day of redemption.

EPHESIANS 4:30

———— ● ————

I pray that You, God, who have begun a
good work in my daughter will complete it
until the day of Jesus Christ.

PHILIPPIANS 1:6

———— ● ————

I pray, Lord, that Your faithfulness will
establish my daughter and guard her from
the evil one.

2 THESSALONIANS 3:3

———— ● ————

I pray that You, God, are able to keep my
daughter from stumbling and to present
her faultless before the presence of Your
glory with exceeding joy.

JUDE 1:24

39

SERVING GOD

Lord God, in accordance with Your perfect word I
pray that my daughter will walk after You and that
she will serve You. Your word is clear that she
cannot serve two masters. Now—at this very
moment—I ask You to honor Your word in the area
of my daughter's service to You. Use Your Holy
Spirit to guide her and direct her in this area of her
life in accordance with Your word which I now
pray. Thank You in Jesus' name. Amen.

**God, in accordance
with Your Word . . .**

I pray that my daughter will walk after You,
the LORD her God, and fear You, and keep
Your commandments and obey Your voice,
and that she shall serve You and hold fast
to You.

DEUTERONOMY 13:4

I pray, God, that my daughter knows that
she cannot serve two masters; for either
she will hate the one and love the other, or
else she will be loyal to the one and despise
the other. She cannot serve You and
mammon.

MATTHEW 6:24

●

I pray that my daughter will love You, the
LORD her God, and walk in all Your ways,
keeping Your commandments, and holding
fast to You, and serving You with all her
heart and with all her soul.

JOSHUA 22:5

●

I pray to You, God, that my daughter will
present her body a living sacrifice, holy,
acceptable to You, which is her reasonable
service. I pray also that she will not be
conformed to this world, but be
transformed by the renewing of her mind,
that she may prove what is that good and
acceptable and perfect will of Yours.

ROMANS 12:1–2

I pray that my daughter will worship You,
the Lord her God, and You only she shall
serve.

MATTHEW 4:10

———————— ● ————————

I pray that my daughter will be kindly
affectionate to others with sisterly love, in
honor giving preference to others; not
lagging in diligence, fervent in spirit,
serving You, Lord; rejoicing in hope,
patient in tribulation, continuing
steadfastly in prayer; distributing to the
needs of the saints, given to hospitality.

ROMANS 12:10–13

———————— ● ————————

I pray, O God, that my daughter shall serve
You, the LORD her God.

EXODUS 23:25

———————— ● ————————

I pray that my daughter will fear You and
walk in all Your ways and love You, and
serve You, the LORD her God, with all her

heart and with all her soul and that she will keep Your commandments and Your statutes which You command her today for her good.

DEUTERONOMY 10:12–13

———— ● ————

I pray that my daughter does not turn aside from following You, LORD, but serves You with all her heart. I pray that she does not turn aside, for then she would go after empty things which cannot profit or deliver, for they are nothing. For You will not forsake her, for Your great name's sake, because it has pleased You to make her Yours.

1 SAMUEL 12:20–22

———— ● ————

I pray that my daughter has been delivered from the law, having died to what she was held by, so that she should serve in the newness of the Spirit and not in the oldness of the letter.

ROMANS 7:6

I pray that my daughter will know You,
God, and serve You with a loyal heart and
with a willing mind; for You search all hearts
and understand all the intent of the thoughts.
If she seeks You, You will be found by her;
but if she forsakes You, You will cast her
off forever.

1 CHRONICLES 28:9

●

I pray that my daughter will serve You,
LORD, with gladness and that she will come
before Your presence with singing. I pray
that she will know that You, Lord, are God
and that it is You who have made her, and
not she herself.

PSALM 100:2–3

40

SICKNESS

Heavenly Father, in accordance with the perfection of Your word I pray that You will heal my daughter of her affliction and restore her health. We need Your help and pray for that important need to be met. It is in the powerful name of Jesus that I pray these prayers to You. Amen.

God, in accordance with Your Word . . .

I pray that You will heal my daughter, O Lord, and she shall be healed. Save her and she shall be saved.

JEREMIAH 17:14

———— ● ————

I pray, God, that You will restore health to my daughter and heal her wounds.

JEREMIAH 30:17

I pray that my daughter will diligently heed Your voice, LORD God, and do what is right in Your sight and give ear to Your commandments and keep all Your statutes, and that You will put no diseases on her.

EXODUS 15:26

I pray, O God, that by Jesus' stripes my daughter is healed, because He was wounded for her transgressions and He was bruised for her iniquities.

ISAIAH 53:5

I pray, God, that You heal all my daughter's diseases and redeem her life from destruction.

PSALM 103:3–4

I pray that Jesus Himself bore my daughter's sins in His own body on the tree, and that she, having died to sin, might live for righteousness—by whose stripes she was healed.

1 PETER 2:24

————— ● —————

I pray that my daughter may prosper in all things and be in health, just as her soul prospers.

3 JOHN 1:2

————— ● —————

I pray, O God, that my daughter remembers that Jesus healed every sickness and every disease among the people.

MATTHEW 9:35

————— ● —————

I pray that the prayer of faith will save my daughter from her sickness and that You, Lord, will raise her up. And if she has committed sins, she will be forgiven.

JAMES 5:15

I pray, Jesus, that power goes out from You
and heals my daughter.

LUKE 6:19

———— ● ————

I pray, God, that You have sent Your word
and healed my daughter and delivered her
from destruction.

PSALM 107:20

———— ● ————

I pray, God, that I am not worthy that You
should come under my roof. But only speak
a word, and my daughter will be healed.

MATTHEW 8:8

41

SPIRITUAL GROWTH

Lord Jesus, there is no more powerful prayer that I can pray than to pray the word of God directly from the pages of the Bible. That is what I now do as I pray for my daughter's spiritual growth. I pray that, as Your word says, she will take heed to herself and keep herself in accordance with Your word. Thank You for honoring Your words that I pray to You now. Amen.

God, in accordance with Your Word . . .

I pray that my daughter will beware, lest there be in her an evil heart of unbelief in departing from the living God. I pray that I will exhort her daily, while it is called "Today," lest she be hardened through the deceitfulness of sin.

HEBREWS 3:12–13

I pray that my daughter does not forget You, the LORD her God, by not keeping Your commandments, Your judgments, and Your statutes which You command her today. I pray that she shall remember the LORD her God, for it is You who gives her the power to get wealth.

DEUTERONOMY 8:11, 18

I pray that my daughter has not forgotten the name of her God, or stretched out her hands to a foreign god. Would You, God, not search this out? For You know the secrets of the heart.

PSALM 44:20–21

I pray that my daughter will take heed to herself, and diligently keep herself, lest she forget the things her eyes have seen, and lest they depart from her heart all the days of her life.

DEUTERONOMY 4:9

I pray, God, that my daughter will be watchful, and strengthen the things which remain, that are ready to die, for she has not found her works perfect before You.

REVELATION 3:2

———— ● ————

I pray, God, that my daughter returns to You, and You will return to her.

MALACHI 3:7

———— ● ————

I pray that my daughter will look diligently lest she fall short of Your grace, God, and lest any root of bitterness spring up causing trouble, and by this she become defiled.

HEBREWS 12:15

———— ● ————

I pray that after my daughter has escaped the pollutions of the world through the knowledge of her Lord and Savior Jesus Christ, that she not become entangled in them and overcome.

2 PETER 2:20

42

STRENGTH

God, I call upon You now to give my daughter more strength than ever before. I pray Your word that You will increase her strength according to Your word and I ask You to do that even as I pray Your word as my prayers for strength for my daughter. In Jesus' precious name I pray. Amen.

God, in accordance
with Your Word . . .

I pray, God, that You give power to my daughter, who is weak, and that You increase her strength.

ISAIAH 40:29

———————— ● ————————

I pray that my daughter shall wait on You, LORD, and that she shall renew her strength. I pray that she shall mount up with wings

like eagles, that she shall run and not be
weary and that she shall walk and not faint.

ISAIAH 40:31

———— • ————

I pray that my daughter will fear not, for
You are with her. I pray that she will be not
dismayed, for You are her God. You will
strengthen her and help her and You will
uphold her with Your righteous right hand.

ISAIAH 41:10

———— • ————

I pray that You, LORD, are my daughter's
light and her salvation. Whom shall she
fear?

PSALM 27:1

———— • ————

I pray, God, that You will strengthen my
daughter according to Your word.

PSALM 119:28

I pray that my daughter will be strong in
You, Lord, and in the power of Your might.
I pray that she will put on the whole armor
of God, that she may be able to stand against
the wiles of the devil. For she does not
wrestle against flesh and blood, but against
principalities, against powers, against the
rulers of the darkness of this age, against
spiritual hosts of wickedness in the heavenly
places.

EPHESIANS 6:10–12

———————— ● ————————

I pray that my daughter will take up Your
whole armor, God, that she may be able to
withstand in the evil day, and having done
all, to stand. I pray that she will stand
therefore, having girded her waist with
truth, having put on the breastplate of
righteousness, and having shod her feet
with the preparation of the gospel of
peace; above all, taking the shield of faith
with which she will be able to quench all
the fiery darts of the wicked one. I pray
also that she will take the helmet of
salvation, and the sword of the Spirit,

which is the word of God, praying always
with all prayer and supplication in the
Spirit.

EPHESIANS 6:13–18

●

I pray that my daughter will be strengthened
with all might, according to Your glorious
power, God.

COLOSSIANS 1:11

●

I pray that my daughter can do all things
through Christ who strengthens her.

PHILIPPIANS 4:13

●

I pray that You, God, will grant my daughter,
according to the riches of Your glory, to be
strengthened with might through Your Spirit.

EPHESIANS 3:16

I pray that You, LORD, are my daughter's rock
and her fortress and her deliverer; her God,
her strength, in whom she will trust; her
shield and the horn of her salvation, her
stronghold. I pray that she will call upon
You, LORD, who are worthy to be praised;
so shall she be saved from her enemies.

PSALM 18:2–3

43

TEMPTED

Jesus, Your word says that You know how to deliver my daughter out of temptations. I pray right now that You will now and forevermore deliver the daughter that I love so much from any temptation that she may encounter. I pray for her in this area, and I trust You to do as Your word promises. In Your name I pray. Amen.

God, in accordance with Your Word . . .

I pray that You, Lord, know how to deliver my daughter out of temptations.

2 PETER 2:9

———— ● ————

I pray that sin shall not have dominion over my daughter, for she is not under law but under grace.

ROMANS 6:14

I pray, Lord, that Your word my daughter has hidden in her heart, that she might not sin against You.

PSALM 119:11

———— ● ————

I pray, Lord, that my daughter will not say when she is tempted, "I am tempted by God"; for You cannot be tempted by evil, nor do You Yourself tempt anyone. For she is tempted when she is drawn away by her own desires and enticed. Then, when desire has conceived, it gives birth to sin; and sin, when it is full-grown, brings forth death. I pray that my daughter will not be deceived.

JAMES 1:13–16

———— ● ————

I pray that no temptation has overtaken my daughter except such as is common to man; but You, God, are faithful and will not allow her to be tempted beyond what she is able, but with the temptation You will also make the way of escape, that she may be able to bear it.

1 CORINTHIANS 10:13

I pray that if my daughter confesses and forsakes her sins she will have mercy.

PROVERBS 28:13

———— ● ————

I pray that if my daughter confesses her sins, You are faithful and just to forgive her sins and to cleanse her from all unrighteousness.

1 JOHN 1:9

———— ● ————

I pray that my daughter does not have a High Priest who cannot sympathize with her weaknesses, but was in all points tempted as she is, yet without sin. Let her therefore come boldly to the throne of grace, that she may obtain mercy and find grace to help in time of need.

HEBREWS 4:15–16

———— ● ————

I pray, Jesus, that You are able to aid my daughter who is tempted.

HEBREWS 2:18

I pray that my daughter will be sober and vigilant; because her adversary the devil walks about like a roaring lion, seeking whom he may devour. I pray that she will resist him, steadfast in the faith, knowing that the same sufferings are experienced by her Christian sisters and brothers in the world.

1 PETER 5:8–9

I pray that my daughter will be strong in You, Lord, and in Your might. I pray that she will put on Your whole armor, that she may be able to stand against the wiles of the devil and that above all, she takes the shield of faith with which she will be able to quench all the fiery darts of the wicked one.

EPHESIANS 6:10–11, 16

I pray, God, that my daughter will resist the devil and he will flee from her.

JAMES 4:7

I pray, God, that He who is in my daughter
is greater than he who is in the world.

1 JOHN 4:4

———— ● ————

I pray, Lord, that my daughter will count it
all joy when she falls into various trials,
knowing that the testing of her faith
produces patience. I pray that blessed is
my daughter who endures temptation; for
when she has been approved, she will
receive the crown of life which You have
promised to those who love You.

JAMES 1:2–3. 12

———— ● ————

I pray that in this my daughter will greatly
rejoice, though now for a little while, if
need be, she has been grieved by various
trials, that the genuineness of her faith,
being much more precious than gold that
perishes, though it is tested by fire, may be
found to praise, honor, and glory at the
revelation of Jesus Christ.

1 PETER 1:6–7

I pray that You, God, are able to keep my daughter from stumbling, and to present her faultless before the presence of Your glory with exceeding joy.

JUDE 1:24

44

TROUBLES

Lord, Your word says that You will allow no more troubles than my daughter can bear. Today, even now, I pray Your word to overcome any troubles my daughter may have. Please honor Your words as my prayers and take care of and strengthen her. It is in the authority of the name of Jesus that I pray. Amen.

God, in accordance
with Your Word . . .

I pray that my daughter shall obtain joy and gladness and that sorrow and sighing shall flee away.

ISAIAH 51:11

—————— • ——————

I pray that my daughter will be anxious for nothing, but in everything by prayer and supplication, with thanksgiving, will let her

requests be made known to You, God, and
Your peace, which surpasses all
understanding, will guard her heart and
mind through Christ Jesus.

PHILIPPIANS 4:6–7

———— ● ————

I pray, God, that my daughter does not
worry about tomorrow, for tomorrow will
worry about its own things.

MATTHEW 6:34

———— ● ————

I pray that all things work together for good
to my daughter who loves You, God,
because she is called according to Your
purpose.

ROMANS 8:28

———— ● ————

I pray that my daughter will be glad and
rejoice in Your mercy, for You have
considered her trouble. You have known
her soul in adversities, and have not shut

her up into the hand of the enemy; You
have set her feet in a wide place.

PSALM 31:7–8

———— ● ————

I pray, God, that You will comfort my
daughter in all her tribulation, that she
may be able to comfort those who are in
any trouble, with the comfort with which
she herself is comforted by You.

2 CORINTHIANS 1:4

———— ● ————

I pray that my daughter's help comes from
You, LORD, who made heaven and earth.

PSALM 121:2

———— ● ————

I pray that my daughter will come boldly
to the throne of grace, that she may obtain
mercy and find grace to help in time of
need.

HEBREWS 4:16

I pray, God, that my daughter will cast all
her cares upon You, for You care for her.

1 PETER 5:7

———— ● ————

I pray, O God, that my daughter always
remembers that You are good, a stronghold
in her day of trouble; and that You know
that she trusts in You.

NAHUM 1:7

———— ● ————

I pray that though my daughter is hard
pressed on every side, she is not crushed;
she is perplexed, but not in despair;
persecuted, but not forsaken; struck down,
but not destroyed.

2 CORINTHIANS 4:8–9

———— ● ————

I pray that my daughter will not let her
heart be troubled. I pray that she believes
in You, God, and also in Jesus.

JOHN 14:1

I pray that though my daughter walks in the midst of trouble, You, God, will revive her. You will stretch out Your hand against the wrath of her enemies, and Your right hand will save her.

PSALM 138:7

I pray, God, that when my daughter passes through the waters, You will be with her. And through the rivers, they shall not overflow her. When she walks through the fire, she shall not be burned, nor shall the flame scorch her.

ISAIAH 43:2

45

WAITING ON GOD

Heavenly Father, I really do believe that the most important thing that I can do is to pray Your very words and thoughts over my daughter. My prayers today will be Your words from Your word. Hear my prayers and help my daughter to wait on You. I pray everything in Jesus' wonderful name. Amen.

God, in accordance
with Your Word . . .

I pray that my daughter has become a partaker of Christ if she holds the beginning of her confidence steadfast to the end.

HEBREWS 3:14

●

I pray that my daughter waits for You, Lord, that her soul waits, and in Your word she does hope.

PSALM 130:5

I pray, God, that my daughter will say in that day: "Behold, this is my God; I have waited for Him, and He will save me. This is the LORD; I have waited for Him. I will be glad and rejoice in His salvation."

ISAIAH 25:9

———— ● ————

I pray, God, that my daughter's soul waits silently for You alone and that her expectation is from You.

PSALM 62:5

———— ● ————

I pray, O God, that my daughter will hold fast to the confession of her hope without wavering, for You who promised are faithful.

HEBREWS 10:23

———— ● ————

I pray that my daughter shall wait on You, LORD, and that she shall renew her strength. I pray also that she shall mount up with

wings like eagles and that she shall run
and not be weary, and walk and not faint.

ISAIAH 40:31

———————— ● ————————

I pray that my daughter's soul waits for
You, LORD, for You are her help and her
shield.

PSALM 33:20

———————— ● ————————

I pray that my daughter will wait on You,
LORD, and that she will be of good courage.
I pray also that You will strengthen her
heart.

PSALM 27:14

46

WORRIED

Most Precious God, I pray Your very words over the worries of my daughter. You have promised to not let her heart be troubled if she will cast her cares on You. Based on Your words I pray that all worry will flee from her and that her joy will return to her. All of my prayers I pray in Jesus' name. Amen.

God, in accordance
with Your Word . . .

I pray, God, that my daughter will not let her heart be troubled.

JOHN 14:1

I pray that my daughter will cast all her cares upon You, God, for You care for her.

1 PETER 5:7

I pray that my daughter will lie down in peace, and sleep; for You alone, O Lord, make her dwell in safety.

PSALM 4:8

———————— ● ————————

I pray that You, God, will keep my daughter in perfect peace, she whose mind is stayed on You, because she trusts in You.

ISAIAH 26:3

———————— ● ————————

I pray, God, that my daughter will let Your peace rule in her heart.

COLOSSIANS 3:15

———————— ● ————————

I pray, Jesus, that Your peace You leave with my daughter and that Your peace You give to her; not as the world gives do You give to her. Let not her heart be troubled, neither let it be afraid.

JOHN 14:27

I pray that my daughter will be anxious for nothing, but in everything by prayer and supplication, with thanksgiving, let her requests be made known to You, God, and Your peace, which surpasses all understanding, will guard her heart and mind in Christ Jesus.

PHILIPPIANS 4:6–7

———— ● ————

I pray, God, that You shall supply all my daughter's needs according to Your riches in glory by Christ Jesus.

PHILIPPIANS 4:19

———— ● ————

I pray that my daughter will not worry about her life, what she will eat or what she will drink; nor about her body, what she will put on. I pray that she will seek first Your kingdom, God, and Your righteousness, and all these things shall be added to her.

MATTHEW 6:25, 33

I pray, Lord, that when my daughter lies down, she will not be afraid. I pray that she will lie down and her sleep will be sweet.

PROVERBS 3:24

———————— ● ————————

I pray that my daughter will say of You, LORD, "He is my refuge and my fortress; my God, in Him I will trust."

PSALM 91:2

———————— ● ————————

I pray, O God, that great peace has my daughter who loves Your law, and nothing can cause her to stumble.

PSALM 119:165

Seminars conducted by Lee Roberts include *Praying God's Will*, *Avoiding Failure in Your Christian Walk*, and *The Businessman, the Salesman, and God!*

More information on these seminars can be obtained by writing Lee Roberts, P.O. Box 671465, Marietta, GA 30067-0025, or by calling 404-956-8550.